LEARNING TO USE SPSSx™

Gilles O. Einstein
Elaine C. Nocks

Furman University

Prentice-Hall, Inc., Englewood Cliffs, New Jersey 07632

Library of Congress Cataloging-in-Publication Data

Einstein, Gilles O. (date)
   Learning to use SPSS˟.

   On t.p. "x" is superscript.
   Includes index.
   1. SPSS X (Computer system) 2. Social
sciences—Data processing. I. Nocks,
Elaine C. (date). II. Title.
HA32.E45 1987   005.3'29   86–30263
ISBN 0–13–528050–8

**To Patty and Julie and to my parents
To Barry and Laurin**

Cover design: Wanda Lubelska
Manufacturing buyer: Barbara Kelly Kittle

© 1987 by Prentice-Hall, Inc.
A Division of Simon & Schuster
Englewood Cliffs, New Jersey 07632

Printed in the United States of America

10 9 8 7 6 5 4 3 2 1

ISBN 0-13-528050-8   01

Prentice-Hall International (UK) Limited, *London*
Prentice-Hall of Australia Pty. Limited, *Sydney*
Prentice-Hall Canada Inc., *Toronto*
Prentice-Hall Hispanoamericana, S.A., *Mexico*
Prentice-Hall of India Private Limited, *New Delhi*
Prentice-Hall of Japan, Inc., *Tokyo*
Prentice-Hall of Southeast Asia Pte. Ltd., *Singapore*
Editora Prentice-Hall do Brasil, Ltda., *Rio de Janeiro*

Contents

Preface

Computer literacy is becoming increasingly indispensible for social science research. As a result, most college and university computer centers have acquired one or more of the major statistical software packages. The Statistical Package for the Social Sciences (SPSS) is among the most powerful and popular of these packages. The most recent revision, known as the SPSS^x Batch System, is a highly convenient and flexible set of statistical programs. Often, however, instructors in research methods and/or statistics courses do not have sufficient time both to teach research design and statistics and also to teach the use of SPSS^x. Our purpose in writing the present book (which is an adaptation of our earlier book *Learning to Use the SPSS Batch System*) is to help new users learn the essentials of SPSS^x quickly and painlessly.

To facilitate rapid and self-directed learning of SPSS^x, we have provided instruction that is as clear and nontechnical as we can make it. We have eliminated much of the complexity in the presently available manuals by omitting rarely used SPSS^x options and procedures and by focusing on the SPSS^x language rather than on statistics. Thus, although this book covers the statistical tests that are essential for a solid foundation in statistics, it is not a statistics text. Instead, it is designed to be used by people who have some background in statistics or to be used in conjunction with a statistics text by students who are enrolled in a statistics course. In short, this manual provides self-contained descriptions of how to use SPSS^x for statistical procedures that are typically encountered in social science research.

The most important feature of this book is its instructional approach. We have included numerous and complete examples in each chapter. In these examples, we present a description of the research problem and design, realistic data sets, complete SPSS^x files, the computer printouts from the SPSS^x programs, and descriptions of these printouts. We illustrate simple methods for performing the analyses and more elaborate variations using the same data. We hope this approach will get you "up and running" with SPSS^x quickly.

In line with our pedagogical orientation, we have tested an earlier version of this book in our sophomore/junior level course in experimental and statistical methods. It was used along with a standard statistics text such that the concepts of design and statistics were taught as usual but students also learned how to use the SPSS^x package. In our experience, students need about two hours of lecture or laboratory time to become familiar with the use of the local computer system and with the basic structure of an SPSS^x program before they are able to perform the procedures on their own. In our courses we do not wish to substitute the use of SPSS^x for an adequate understanding of statistical theory. Our students are still required to perform the traditional assignments by hand, but in addition, they learn to transfer their understanding of statistics to the more efficient and powerful use of the computer for data analysis. In fact, we have found that using a statistical package reinforces a solid understanding of statistics and often has the added benefit of encouraging reluctant students to learn more about computers and programming. We have also used this book with undergraduates who are conducting independent research. With minimal instruction, these students are soon performing thorough statistical analyses on their own data.

We are grateful to all of our students and colleagues at Furman University who used the previous book, providing us with valuable and encouraging feedback for the writing of this one. We are indebted to Lib Nanney, who has sustained us through the writing of both books; her contributions to the manuscript go well beyond typing. Furman University Computer Center director James Runde has been an accessible consultant and has provided us with the full resources of the center. The editorial and publication staff of Prentice-Hall, Inc., reviewers Richard Wright, of Northern Michigan University, and Bernard Frank, of Kansas State University, and the personnel at SPSS, Inc., have also provided important assistance in the preparation of the manuscript. Parts of this book were written and tested at the University of New Mexico while the first author was on sabbatical. We wish to thank Henry Ellis, Tim Goldsmith, and Dick Harris for their assistance in obtaining relevant information and computer access there.

Finally, we would like to acknowledge our deep affection and appreciation for our own mentors in research and statistics: Bill Battig of the University of Colorado, Burt Cohen of Lafayette College, and Chet Insko of the University of North Carolina. They not only instilled in us an appreciation of the importance and challenge of the scientific method but also taught us how to interpret a five-way analysis of variance!

Our efforts and contributions have been truly collaborative. To represent that equality, we have randomly determined the order of authorship.

Introduction

SPSSˣ AS A LANGUAGE

The purpose of this manual is to provide you with an efficient means of learning a very powerful computer language that can be used to perform most statistical procedures that a social scientist is likely to encounter. Although many computer languages have been developed for this purpose over the years, we have chosen SPSSˣ, the revised version of the Statistical Package for the Social Sciences (SPSS), because it is widely available and covers a broad spectrum of statistical procedures. Also, SPSSˣ was designed to be understood and used by persons having little background in computers.

SPSSˣ is a computer software package—that is, a set of computer programs written by experts for other individuals to use with their own data. It was developed specifically for analyzing data from social science research. In contrast to more general languages such as BASIC, Pascal, and FORTRAN, the SPSSˣ language is much simpler because of its narrower focus. As with any language, however, both the vocabulary (commands) and the grammar (rules for ordering these commands) are essential for effective communication. Hence, in reading this manual, you should pay particular attention to both the commands and their proper format and location in the SPSS^x program. As you become familiar with the SPSS^x language, you will find that directing the computer to perform the statistical analyses that are appropriate for your data is very logical and simple.

THIS MANUAL COMPARED WITH THE SPSS^x USER'S GUIDE

Our goal is *not* to provide you with an exhaustive description of SPSS^x. Such a description is available in the *SPSS^x User's Guide* by SPSS Inc. (McGraw-Hill, 1983; 1986). Occasionally, we will refer you to specific sections in that manual. We want to help you learn how to use SPSS^x for common, relatively straightforward procedures. Our goal is to have you master the logic without being overwhelmed by all of the choices available to you. Thus, we have included in our manual the primary control commands used in all SPSS^x analyses and the statistical procedures that are typically used by social science students (on data obtained from surveys, tests, and simple experiments). For the sake of clarity, we have intentionally omitted several infrequently used and complex options and variations. However, as you increase your basic understanding of SPSS^x and as the need for more complex statistical methods arises, you should investigate these options in the aforementioned manual.

Although you need have little or no previous experience with computers, you must already be somewhat familiar with the basic statistical concepts that are covered in this manual. Our purpose is not to teach you statistics but rather to teach you how to use SPSS^x. We describe how to create SPSS^x programs that will perform many statistical tests. Your knowledge of statistics, however, is necessary for determining which statistical procedures are appropriate for your data and for interpreting the results of your SPSS^x output.

GAINING ACCESS TO SPSS^x ON YOUR COMPUTER

SPSS^x consists of a set of programs stored in the memory of the computer. To communicate with these programs, you will need to use input and output devices (see Figure 1.1). Usually, the input device is a computer terminal that contains a keyboard and viewing screen. You will use the keyboard to type in your data and instructions (commands) for analyzing the data. These instructions and data are entered on lines (also called records) that are generally 80 characters long. Characters are individual letters, numbers, other symbols, or blank spaces. A set of command lines and data lines will compose your personal SPSS^x file. When the instructions from your file are executed by the computer, they are, in fact, communicat-

Terminal

Your commands and
data are entered
here.

Central Processing Unit
(CPU)

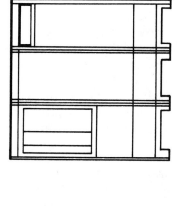

All processing and storage of information
occurs in the CPU of the computer. The
SPSS˟ program and any files that you create
are stored here. The CPU also processes and
analyzes your data.

Output Device

Line Printer

Your results are
printed out here.

FIGURE 1.1 Components of a Computer System

3

ing with the SPSS[x] program package. The results (or output) are sent to an appropriate output device—typically a line printer.*

To get the computer to read your SPSS[x] commands and your data lines, you will have to learn how to create and store files on your computer system. Because computer equipment varies greatly from one facility to another, we will not be able to give you the specific instructions for doing this. You will therefore need to find out how your particular system works before you can begin typing in the SPSS[x] commands. Consult the appropriate personnel in your computer center to determine what input and output devices are available and how to create, edit, and store files on your system.

EFFECTIVE USE OF THIS MANUAL

In this chapter, we have given you an overview of the text and of the file creation skills that are necessary to use SPSS[x]. In Chapter 2, which you must read next, we present a summary of the important commands of typical SPSS[x] programs and the format and organization of these commands. We also suggest a method of entering your data. Once you have described the nature of your data to SPSS[x] through the commands, you are ready to perform statistical analyses on these data. Before you go on, however, we recommend that you read Chapter 3, where some additional SPSS[x] commands are described. Among other things, these will enable you to provide variable and value labels for your printout, modify the data or select particular cases for analysis, account for missing data, and store and retrieve data files.

Chapters 4 through 12 contain specific statistical procedures and need not be read in any particular order. As shown in Figure 1.2, these procedures are independent of one another, and each one was written to be understandable after you have read Chapters 2 and 3. These chapters contain complete examples for each procedure, including a research problem, a hypothetical set of data, a listing of all necessary commands, and a printout of results. An additional example is inserted to illustrate common variations or options. Chapter 13 discusses common errors made by SPSS[x] users—how to find them and how to correct them. Finally, Chapter 14 describes additional capabilities of SPSS[x]. After you feel comfortable with using the SPSS[x] procedures described in this manual, we encourage you to explore these additional SPSS[x] features.

---

*On many computer systems the output of your program is first sent to what is called a *display* file. Once your SPSS[x] program is executed, you then have the option of viewing the results of the program at your terminal before you request a printout of the results. This is a convenient option that enables you to check quickly for warnings and errors in your program. You can then make the necessary corrections in your SPSS[x] file before requesting a printout of the results. You should ask your local computer personnel about how to access and/or print display files.

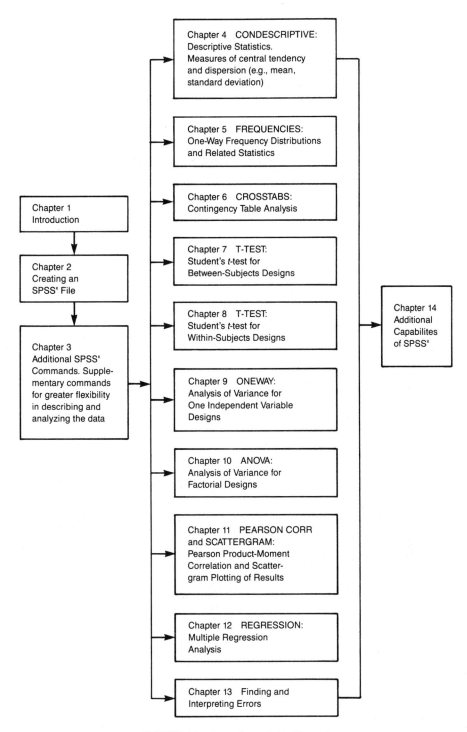

FIGURE 1.2 Overview of the Manual

2

Creating an SPSS× File

OVERVIEW OF AN SPSS× FILE

Although SPSS× allows data to be entered or accessed in several ways, we have chosen here to present the method in which data are entered as part of your SPSS× file. This will help you learn the logic of SPSS× files and will prepare you for other methods of data entry to be described in Chapter 3. It is useful to think of your file (the one you will be typing into the computer) as consisting of three kinds of information:

1. A few non-SPSS× commands (called Job Control Language, or JCL, commands) that are necessary to interact with your local computer
2. SPSS× commands that describe the data and cause statistical analyses to be performed
3. The data you have collected, usually in the form of one or more lines of numerically coded values for each subject or case examined

The arrangement of the three types of information for your SPSS× file is shown in a sample file in Figure 2.1. (Do not worry about the specific SPSS× commands or their functions yet.)

FIGURE 2.1   Sample SPSS^x File

(Column number	`123456789...)`
	↓
JCL commands	`JOB...`
	`EXEC SPSSX` (or **RUN SPSSX** in some systems)...
SPSS^x	
commands	`TITLE "CORRELATION OF HEIGHT WITH WEIGHT"`
	`DATA LIST  /HEIGHT 1-2 WEIGHT 4-6`
	`PEARSON CORR  HEIGHT WITH WEIGHT`
	`BEGIN DATA`
Data lines	`60  98`
	`66 135`
	`72 200`
	`.`
	`.`
	`.`
	`68 235`
SPSS^x	
commands	`END DATA`
	`FINISH`
JCL command	`END OF JOB` (or **EOJ** in some systems)...

JCL COMMANDS

Although the JCL commands vary from one system to another, their purposes are similar. As shown in Figure 2.1, the first JCL command is a JOB statement. The functions of this statement are (1) to identify the beginning of your program and (2) to provide personal identification that allows the computer to verify that you are a legitimate user of the system. The EXEC statement (or RUN statement in some systems) informs the computer that you are using the SPSS^x language and requests access to the SPSS^x program. These two commands precede any SPSS^x commands. The END OF JOB (or EOJ) command is the last command in your file and indicates to the computer that this is the end of your program. Note that these commands differ in format for different computer systems and that you will have to obtain the specific details of the JCL statements from your instructor or computer center personnel.

To give you a concrete example of what these statements might look like, we have listed one possible form for the JCL commands. This example illustrates the form for a particular computer system; you will have to obtain the appropriate commands for your system.

```
: JOB name/password.account;OUTCLASS=6
: EXEC SPSSX.PUB.SPSSX

(SPSSx program)

: EOJ
```

A specific example of the first JCL command with the name, password, and account follows:

```
:JOB JONES/LIB123.PSYCHOL;OUTCLASS=6
```

You will need to use JCL commands in every program that you write. Thus, you may want to list the JCL commands for *your* system on the following lines:

```
Initial JCL command(s)

_____

_____

_____


Ending JCL command(s)

_____

_____


Do not list your actual password here because others may use your book. You should
memorize your password and keep a copy of it in a safe place.
```

BASIC SPSS^x COMMANDS

Figure 2.2 lists the basic commands that usually appear in an SPSS^x file. Notice that only a few commands are needed in a simple analysis in which there are no missing data, no additional data transformations, and no reason for elaborate descriptive material on the printout. From this list of commands, you can see that the order of the instructions to the computer follows a logical pattern. For example, the names and locations of your variables—the DATA LIST command—must appear before your actual data. It is important to note the relative *order* of the commands because a proper logical sequence must be followed.

PREPARING AND CODING YOUR DATA FOR SPSS^x

Within the SPSS^x file, it will be necessary to indicate the names of the variables and their locations in the data line. This arrangement of the

FIGURE 2.2 Basic SPSS^x Commands

RELATIVE LOCATION IN FILE	NAME OF COMMAND	FUNCTION OF THE COMMAND
1	TITLE	Provides a title for your printout
2	DATA LIST	Tells the computer the names of your variables and the column locations for each variable
3	Procedure command (e.g., ANOVA)	Defines the particular statistical analysis to be performed
4	BEGIN DATA	Tells the computer that the next line it reads is data from the first subject or case
5	Data lines	At least one line of data for each subject or case is presented here for the computer to read
6	END DATA	Tells the computer that the preceding line was the last line of data from the last subject or case
7	FINISH	Tells the computer that all commands for the SPSS^x job have been entered

values on a line is specified in the DATA LIST command, which will be discussed later in this chapter. In preparing your data, you should think about the scores or variables that you want to include for each case or subject. What constitutes a case varies from study to study, but basically a case is an individual unit that you have chosen to measure. For example, a case may be a subject in an experiment or an individual in a survey. This is the way we have generally used the concept of case in this manual; however, cases do not necessarily refer to specific individuals. For example, if you were interested in the average family income in different countries, each country would be a case. If you were interested in the yearly number of traffic fatalities from 1920 to the present, each year would be a case. In addition to defining what a case is in your particular research, you should identify the important variables that you wish to analyze. Then you will have to decide (1) how you will code (represent) the values of these variables for each case and (2) the column locations for each variable.

Most SPSS^x procedures require that data be in the form of numerical values. (Some procedures can accommodate alphabetic codes, or recoding from alphabetic to numeric codes can be done.) Thus you will need to devise a coding scheme before you begin to type in the data. As an illustration, suppose that you have performed an experiment on rats in which you varied the dosage level of a drug in two ways—low and high. You have randomly assigned five subjects (cases) to each drug level. (In a real experiment, you might use many more subjects, but we wish to keep the example simple.) For each subject, you collected three measures of activity—Score

FIGURE 2.3   Data Sheet for Drug Study

SUBJECT	DRUG LEVEL	SCORE 1	SCORE 2	SCORE 3
01	Low	2	3.6	12.06
02	Low	14	2.4	2.50
03	Low	12	.5	1.60
04	Low	3	.1	1.80
05	Low	4	1.6	19.65
06	High	16	2.6	13.64
07	High	25	3.1	10.55
08	High	13	4.2	5.40
09	High	11	5.3	7.36
10	High	9	1.4	11.10

1, Score 2, and Score 3. Your longhand score sheet might resemble Figure 2.3.

To establish a coding scheme for the drug experiment, you might let a low dosage equal 1 and a high dosage equal 2. Having decided on a coding scheme, you are ready to type your data on the lines in your SPSS^x file. Because the values of Score 1, Score 2, and Score 3 are already numeric, these can be typed in exactly as they are.

Considerable flexibility is allowed in preparing data lines. For example, you may or may not want to type in an identification number for each subject. Furthermore, spaces (blank columns) are not needed between the values of the variables, but you may wish to use them to make your data lines easier to read. You can arrange the data on a line in whatever way seems most logical to you, but you *must* use that same form for each subject or case.

You must follow a few rules in typing your data:

1. Only one subject or case may appear on a given data line. In other words, the data for two subjects or cases cannot be typed onto the same line.
2. Values for variables must line up in the same columns for all subjects or cases. This means three things:
    a. You must consistently devote enough column space on a line to accommodate the largest value (greatest number of columns needed by any subject's score) of that variable. For example, in Figure 2.3, you must always allow two columns for Score 1 even though some subjects' scores are a single digit. You should leave the first column blank for cases in which Score 1 occupies only one column.
    b. When subjects' scores require different amounts of column space, they must be lined up according to the rightmost column within the space allocated for that score (i.e., right justified). In other words, if you allow two columns for Score 1 in Figure 2.3, then numbers in the first column will be read as tens and numbers in the second column will be read as

ones. Thus, arrangements A and B as follows would cause different interpretations of your data.

	A	B
	2	2
	14	14
	12	12
	3	3

In arrangement A, which is right justified, the first and last lines would be read as 2 and 3, respectively. In arrangement B, the first and last lines would be read as 20 and 30, respectively.

   c. The decimal place should be in the same column for each variable. For example

5.40	
10.65	Valid
110.20	
5.4	
10.65	Invalid
110.2	

3. Any number of data lines per case or subject is allowed.
4. If more than one line is used, a value of a variable cannot be "split" between two lines:

13.64	Valid
13.6	Invalid
4	

Two valid data files for the drug experiment are shown in Figures 2.4 and 2.5. There are several things to notice in Figure 2.4.

FIGURE 2.4   Contents of Data File for Drug Study

```
(Column 1.........11)
      ↓         ↓
      1 23.612.06
      1142.4 2.50
      112 .5 1.60
      1 3 .1 1.80
      1 41.619.65
      2162.613.64
      2253.110.55
      2134.2 5.40
      2115.3 7.36
      2 91.411.10
          ↑  ↑
        Decimals are in
        the same column
```

FIGURE 2.5   Alternative Data File for Drug Study

```
(Column 1............14)
     ↓            ↓
     1   2 3.6 12.06
     1 14 2.4  2.50
     1 12  .5  1.60
     1  3  .1  1.80
     1  4 1.6 19.65
     2 16 2.6 13.64
     2 25 3.1 10.55
     2 13 4.2  5.40
     2 11 5.3  7.36
     2  9 1.4 11.10
            ↑   ↑
         Decimals are in
         the same column
```

1. We have chosen arbitrarily to begin in the first column with the code for the dosage level, omitting an identification number for each subject.
2. We have typed the values of the variables without leaving spaces between them.
3. All decimals are lined up, as is the rightmost column of each value.

Figure 2.5 shows an alternative way of setting up the same file with spaces between the values of each variable. Although it is less efficient, you may want to enter your values in this way to make it more readable for you—the computer doesn't care!

When you have finished typing in your data, look over the whole file to make sure that everything is lined up and that you do not have any stray or uninterpretable characters (e.g., the letter *O* in place of the number *0*). Accuracy is crucial because the computer will not, for the most part, be able to tell you if you have entered the data correctly.

CODING YOUR DATA: ANOTHER EXAMPLE

As another example, consider an exercise survey in which you collected the following information from a sample of 200 people:

1. Respondent's sex
2. Age in years
3. Education (high school or less, some college, college degree, postgraduate work)
4. Income (under 10,000; 10,000 to 19,999; 20,000 to 29,999; 30,000 to 49,999; 50,000 or more)

5. Weight (in pounds)
6. Amount of weekly exercise (in hours)

Because it is generally best to give numeric codes to your data, you need to plan ahead for these codes. You might use a plan like the following one for the preceding example:

1. Sex: M = 1, F = 2
2. Age: (already numeric)
3. Education: high school or less = 1
    some college = 2
    college degree = 3
    postgraduate = 4
4. Income: under 10,000 = 1
    10,000 to 19,999 = 2
    20,000 to 29,999 = 3
    30,000 to 49,999 = 4
    50,000 or more = 5
5. Weight: (already numeric)
6. Amount of weekly exercise: (already numeric)

Thus your data sheet might look like Figure 2.6. A valid SPSS^x data file based on the data in Figure 2.6 appears in Figure 2.7. Notice in Figure 2.7 that we have arbitrarily chosen not to put spaces (blank columns) between our variables and to omit an identification number for each subject.

Although most SPSS^x procedures require a numeric coding scheme, there are times when you might want to use letters and/or a combination of letters and numbers to represent the values of your variables. This is known as an *alphanumeric* coding scheme. For example, rather than coding males as 1s and females as 2s, you may want to use the codes M and F, respectively. This is a valid option with SPSS^x, and if you choose this method, you will have to pay particular attention to the references to alpha-

FIGURE 2.6   Data Sheet for Exercise Survey

RESPONDENT	SEX	AGE	EDUCATION	INCOME	EXERCISE
1	1	34	4	3	7
2	2	27	3	3	11
3	2	47	3	5	2
4	1	55	2	4	1
.	.	.	.	.	.
.	.	.	.	.	.
.	.	.	.	.	.
200	1	32	3	2	3

FIGURE 2.7   Data File for Exercise Survey

```
(Column 1.....7)
        ↓     ↓
        13443 7
        2273311
        24735 2
        15524 1
          .

          .

          .
        13232 3
```

---

numeric codes in the descriptions of the DATA LIST command (this chapter) and the RECODE command (Chapter 3).

CODING YOUR DATA WITHOUT TYPING IN DECIMAL POINTS

Until now we have been showing you examples in which the decimal points are typed into the data file. This, however, is not necessary. A coding option that is available to you when you are creating your data lines is to omit the decimal points entirely. This is a very efficient option because it reduces the number of characters that you have to type into the data lines. To use this format, follow all the rules described previously but omit the decimal point. For example, the decimal point in Figure 2.4 could be eliminated to yield the data file shown in Figure 2.8.

Note that the *implied decimal points* (between columns 4 and 5 and between columns 7 and 8) must be indicated on your DATA LIST com-

FIGURE 2.8   Data File for Drug Study
with Implied Decimal Points

```
(Column 1.......9)
        ↓       ↓
        1 2361206
        11424 250
        112 5 160
        1 3 1 180
        1 4161965
        216261364
        225311055
        21342 540
        21153 736
        2 9141110
```

---

mand. The format for doing this is described in the DATA LIST section of this chapter.

For the sake of clarity and simplicity, we have chosen to include the decimal points in most examples in this book. In spite of this, if you feel comfortable with implied decimal points, we urge you to use them because they do save typing time.

WHERE TO TYPE THE DATA LINES

There are two methods of typing in your data:

1. *Within-File Method*: Data are typed directly within your SPSS^x file.
2. *Separate-File Method*: Data are typed and stored in a separate file.

The Within-File Method will be used in this chapter and in most examples in this manual because it allows you to see the data along with the SPSS^x commands. Figures 2.1, 2.10, and 2.12 illustrate this method.

The Separate-File Method is an often-used (and equally appropriate) alternative to including the data lines within your SPSS^x file. It involves creating separate files for your SPSS^x commands (SPSS^x command file) and your data lines (data file) and storing these two files under different names. This method is often preferred when there are very large data sets that might be awkward to deal with as you modify your SPSS^x program commands. It is also used when the data are purchased or obtained from some outside source and arrive as an intact file (already on disk or magnetic tape). In this situation, you must tell the computer where to find your data. This requires some changes in your SPSS^x commands. The necessary instructions for using the Separate-File Method are described in Chapter 3 with the description of the FILE HANDLE command.

OVERVIEW OF SPSS^x COMMAND FORMAT

Now that you have a general idea of what your SPSS^x file is going to look like and how to type in your data, you need to learn how to complete the specifications of the SPSS^x commands of the file to fit your data. Each SPSS^x command occupies at least one line in your file. The line is divided into two parts, each with a different purpose.

1. Beginning in column 1 is the *command keyword* or the name of the command (e.g., TITLE or DATA LIST).
2. Following that keyword, and separated from it by at least one blank space, are the *specifications* or instructions specific to your data. If you have more infor-

mation than will fit on one line, continue the instructions on the next line, always indenting at least one column to indicate continuation.

For readability, we have usually skipped two or three spaces (blank columns) between the command keyword and the specification field. Similarly, our indenting and other spacing choices have been made on the basis of visual clarity. We encourage you to use similar flexibility in spacing to enhance the readability of your program. Just remember:

Always begin the command keyword in column 1 and always skip at least one space between it and the specifications. To continue on succeeding lines, indent at least one space on each continuation line.

For example:

```
Columns
123456...
↓   ↓
TITLE "CORRELATON OF HEIGHT WITH WEIGHT"
```

Note that TITLE is the command keyword. It is followed by a space and the actual name to be used (specification). You may, if you wish, leave more spaces between the command keyword and the specifications as shown:

```
Columns
123456...
↓   ↓
TITLE  "CORRELATION OF HEIGHT WITH WEIGHT"
```

Complete accuracy is essential for the program to run. Therefore, you must *type the commands and specifications exactly as they are presented in this manual*—with appropriate spaces and punctuation. If you do make a mistake, an error message will appear on a printout telling you what needs to be corrected. If you get such a message, go over your command lines very carefully, comparing them with the examples given here, to find the error. Some common errors are described in Chapter 13.

DETAILS OF BASIC SPSS^x COMMANDS

We are now going to describe the specific format and functions of the SPSS^x commands. Remember to begin the command keyword in column 1 and space accordingly as described previously.

TITLE Command

```
TITLE  "ANALYSIS OF ACTIVITY SCORES"
```

This command provides a descriptive title that will appear on your printout. After typing in TITLE, you may give any title you like. You should enclose the title in quotation marks (or apostrophes), and you may use up to 60 characters. For example,

```
TITLE  "ANALYSIS OF ACTIVITY SCORES FOR VARYING DOSAGE LEVELS"
```

DATA LIST Command

```
DATA LIST   /DRUG 1 SCORE1 2-3 SCORE2 4-6 SCORE3 7-11
```

This is the command that will tell the computer exactly how to read the data from your study. Before you write this command, you should have decided exactly how your data will be typed into the computer. You will also need to provide short names—*no more than eight characters*—for each variable in the list. The first character of a variable name must be alphabetic, the remaining characters can be alphabetic and/or numeric, and no spaces can occur within the name.

Designates the beginning of the descriptions of the data lines. It is sometimes preceded by other information as described later.

DRUG 1

DRUG is the abbreviated name that we have given to the first variable on the line. In this case, it stands for the dosage level of the drug. The number *1* specifies the column in which the value of that variable is to be read. Thus DRUG 1 tells the computer to read the value of a variable called DRUG in column 1.

SCORE1 2-3

Tells the computer to read the value of a variable called SCORE1 in columns 2 and 3.

SCORE2 4-6

Tells the computer to read the value of a variable called SCORE2 in columns 4 through 6.

SCORE3 7-11

Tells the computer to read the value of a variable called SCORE3 in columns 7 through 11.

You can see that these specifications accurately reflect the way that our sample data of Figure 2.4 are typed. *Remember that you must count a column for each of the decimal points* that are actually typed on the data lines. If you have implied decimal points (i.e., you have not typed the decimal points) in your data file, you must indicate this in your DATA LIST command. This is done by including the number of decimal places (the number of digits to the right of the implied decimal point) with the appropriate variable name. Based on the data file in Figure 2.8, the appropriate format for the DATA LIST command is

```
DATA LIST   /DRUG 1 SCORE1 2-3 SCORE2 4-5 (1) SCORE3 6-9 (2)
```

Note that the number of decimal places is enclosed within parentheses and is placed after the column numbers for the appropriate variable. In the preceding example, the value in column 5 for SCORE2 will be read as tenths. Similarly, for SCORE3, the value in column 8 will be read as tenths, and the value in column 9 will be read as hundredths.

We will now look at a slightly more complicated DATA LIST statement to see a few variations and shortcuts you might find useful.

```
DATA LIST   RECORDS=3/1 SEX 5 RACE 6 (A) VAR1 TO VAR9 7-15
            /2 SCORE1 TO SCORE10 1-20/3 TIME 1-3 Q1 TO Q4 4-7
```

Specifying more than one line of data.   Here we are specifying three lines of data (RECORDS=3) for each subject or case. The keyword RECORDS is needed only when the data for each case require more than one line. These lines are then marked off as /1, /2, and /3. After /1, the variable names (and column locations) are listed for the variables that appear on the first data line. Similarly, the variable names (and column locations) for the second and third data lines are listed after /2 and /3, respectively. You might also notice that we do not want the computer to read anything until column 5 of the first data line (columns 1 to 4 may contain a case or subject identification code that is not to be dealt with in the analysis).

Providing for alphabetic codes.   The code (A) designates that RACE has been coded with a letter instead of a number. For example. you may have coded RACE with the letters B (Black), C (Caucasian), H (Hispanic), and so on.

Shortening the variable list.   You may use the keyword TO as a shorter way of naming a sequence of numbered variables that have the same prefix. Any convenient prefix will do. We have illustrated several. VAR1 TO VAR9 indicates to the computer that there are nine values to be read (VAR1, VAR2, VAR3, . . . VAR9). Similarly, Q1 TO Q4 might refer to answers on questions 1, 2, 3, and 4 of a survey. Note that a series of variables may be listed with the TO method only if they occupy columns of equal length. Thus VAR1 TO VAR9 7-15 indicates that nine columns are used for nine variables, beginning in column 7 and each occupying one column. SCORE1 TO SCORE10 1-20 indicates that 10 variables occupy 20 columns, each variable taking 2 columns. If a variable in the middle of a series of variables needs a different amount of column space, the list must be broken (e.g., SCORE1 TO SCORE5 1-10 SCORE6 11-13 SCORE7 TO SCORE10 14-21).

You may use more than one line for the DATA LIST command. Simply indent at least one space on subsequent lines to show the continuation. Within this restriction, you may arrange subsequent lines of the DATA LIST command in whatever form is sensible to you. For example

```
DATA LIST  RECORDS=3
          /1 SEX 5 RACE 6 (A) VAR1 TO VAR9 7-15
          /2 SCORE1 TO SCORE10 1-20
          /3 TIME 1-3 Q1 TO Q4 4-7
```

We have described the format of the DATA LIST command when data are entered in the same way for each subject or case, that is, with values of variables being located in the same columns or lines for each case (as described in the section on data entry). There are other choices (e.g., freefield format), and these would necessitate changes in the format of the DATA LIST command. (You can refer to these in the *SPSS^x User's Guide* indexed under the keywords FREE or LIST.)

Procedure Commands, OPTIONS, and STATISTICS

Procedure commands cause the computer to read the data and perform the desired statistical analyses. Although numerous statistical procedures are available to you in the SPSS^x package, in this manual we have chosen to present only the most commonly used procedures. (See Figure 2.9.) Each of these procedures, some with their own sets of related OPTIONS and STATISTICS, will be presented separately in Chapters 4 to 12 of this book. For now, we will give you one example—Pearson product-moment correlation—to illustrate the form of these three commands.

```
PEARSON CORR  SCORE1 WITH SCORE2
OPTIONS  6
STATISTICS  1 2
```

FIGURE 2.9 Some SPSS^x Statistical Procedures

```
CONDESCRIPTIVE
FREQUENCIES
CROSSTABS
T-TEST
ONEWAY
ANOVA
PEARSON CORR
REGRESSION
```

The OPTIONS and STATISTICS commands allow you to request any or all of a series of numbered choices related to the procedure. Here, OPTIONS 6 with PEARSON CORR requests the printing of only the nonredundant correlation coefficients. STATISTICS 1 with PEARSON CORR asks for variable means and standard deviations. STATISTICS 2 asks for cross-product deviations and covariance for each pair of variables. If you do not wish to use any of the OPTIONS or STATISTICS, omit these command lines. (You may omit one or both commands.) If you wish to use some but not all of the OPTIONS or STATISTICS, list the appropriate numbers—separated by spaces or commas—with at least one space separating the numbers from the command keyword. For example

```
OPTIONS  2 4 6
STATISTICS  1 3 5
```

In some cases, you can request all of the available OPTIONS or STATISTICS by typing the word ALL:

```
OPTIONS  ALL
STATISTICS  ALL
```

Two of the procedures covered in this book (FREQUENCIES and REGRESSION) do not use the OPTIONS and STATISTICS commands but have other methods for requesting options and statistics.

BEGIN DATA Command

```
BEGIN DATA
```

This command is required when the data are included within your program. It *always immediately precedes* the first data line.

END DATA Command

```
END DATA
```

This command is required when the data are included within your program. It *always immediately follows* the last data line. (As described in Chapter 3, other SPSS^x commands may follow the END DATA command.)

FINISH Command

```
FINISH
```

This is the last line in your SPSS^x file and signals the end of the SPSS^x commands to the computer. No further SPSS^x commands should follow it. It is optional, but we have chosen to use it for clarity.

FIGURE 2.10   SPSS^x File for Drug Study

```
JOB...
EXEC SPSSX...                 (JCL commands for your computer system)
TITLE    "ANALYSIS OF ACTIVITY SCORES"
DATA LIST     /DRUG 1 SCORE1 2-3 SCORE2 4-6 SCORE3 7-11
Procedure                     (Fill this in after reading later chapters.)
BEGIN DATA
1 23.612.06
1142.4 2.50
112 .5 1.60
1 3 .1 1.80
1 41.619.65
2162.613.64
2253.110.55
2134.2 5.40
2115.3 7.36
2 91.411.10
END DATA
FINISH
END OF JOB...                 (JCL command for your computer system)
```

USING THE SPSS^x FILE: THE DRUG STUDY

Using the commands in Figure 2.2 and the data in Figure 2.4, you might try to write an SPSS^x file for the drug study. After you have written the file, compare your file with the one in Figure 2.10 to see how closely your program agrees with the one that we wrote.

ANOTHER EXAMPLE OF A TYPICAL SPSS^x FILE: VISUAL PREFERENCE EXPERIMENT

Assume that you have conducted an experiment to determine if newborn infants prefer patterned or plain stimuli. In the study, 14 infants were presented with both plain and patterned figures. The amount of time spent looking at each type of stimulus was measured. In addition, the sex of the infants and their ages (in days) were recorded. The data sheet for this experiment appears in Figure 2.11, and the SPSS^x file is presented in Figure 2.12. To test yourself, try to write the SPSS^x file before you look at Figure 2.12.

With the commands presented in this chapter, you are now prepared to turn to one of the procedures chapters (4 to 12) and construct an SPSS^x file to analyze your data. As soon as you are comfortable with your basic knowledge of the SPSS^x program format, however, you should familiarize

FIGURE 2.11   Data Sheet for Visual Preference Experiment

SUBJECT NUMBER	SEX[a]	AGE[b]	TIME VIEWING PATTERNED FIGURE[c]	TIME VIEWING PLAIN FIGURE[c]
01	1	3	15	7
02	1	7	13	8
03	1	4	17	9
04	1	6	10	11
05	1	6	14	7
06	1	5	23	10
07	1	4	18	6
08	2	5	16	9
09	2	3	9	7
10	2	4	14	12
11	2	7	21	6
12	2	7	13	9
13	2	6	17	7
14	2	5	12	10

[a]Code for sex: male = 1, female = 2.
[b]Age was measured in days.   [c]Time was measured in seconds.

FIGURE 2.12 SPSS[x] File for Visual Preference Experiment

```
JOB...
EXEC SPSSX...              (JCL commands for your computer system)
TITLE    "VISUAL PREFERENCE EXPERIMENT"
DATA LIST    /SNUM 1-2 SEX 4 AGE 6 PATTERN 8-9 PLAIN 11-12
Procedure*                (Fill this in after reading later chapters.)
BEGIN DATA
01 1 3 15  7
02 1 7 13  8
03 1 4 17  9
04 1 6 10 11
05 1 6 14  7
06 1 5 23 10
07 1 4 18  6
08 2 5 16  9
09 2 3  9  7
10 2 4 14 12
11 2 7 21  6
12 2 7 13  9
13 2 6 17  7
14 2 5 12 10
END DATA
FINISH
END OF JOB...             (JCL command for your computer system)
```

*If you would like to practice typing your commands into a file and executing your program, insert the statement

CONDESCRIPTIVE AGE PATTERN PLAIN

as the procedure on the line between the DATA LIST and BEGIN DATA lines. As you will see in Chapter 4, this command causes the computer to calculate descriptive statistics (e.g., means and standard deviations) for the variables AGE, PATTERN, and PLAIN.

yourself with the additional SPSS^x commands presented in Chapter 3. These commands are routinely used in data analysis to improve description (e.g., with variable names and value labels) and to allow for a variety of transformations of the data (e.g., recoding, performing computations, and selecting subsets of cases for analysis). You will also learn about other methods of accessing and storing data.

3

Additional SPSSˣ Commands

OVERVIEW OF ADDITIONAL COMMANDS

The SPSSˣ commands described in this chapter will provide you with powerful tools for analyzing your data. The first set of commands that we describe will enable you to perform transformations on your data, select different subgroups of cases or subjects for analysis, and provide more detailed information on the printout about the variables. Figure 3.1 lists these commands along with the commands discussed in Chapter 2. (Because you are likely to refer to this figure frequently, it is reprinted on the last page of the manual for your convenience.) Later in this chapter we will also describe several file communication commands (see Figure 3.4), which, among other things, will allow you to store, access, and use your data in different ways. Do not be concerned about the details of the commands yet. At this point, you need only a general idea of what commands are available and how these commands fit into the basic logic of an SPSSˣ file. An awareness of the functions of these commands will enable you to gain the maximum benefits of SPSSˣ. For example, by realizing that you can use the COMPUTE command to convert your raw data to percentages, you can avoid the tedious and time-consuming task of converting your scores by hand.

As you examine the commands listed in Figure 3.1, realize that

1. Most commands are optional and can be used or omitted as you wish to achieve certain kinds of results. Certain commands such as the DATA LIST command are required under most circumstances.
2. Each command has a specific name (e.g., VARIABLE LABELS) that must be used and spelled correctly whenever you want the computer to perform the associated function.
3. Although we have listed the SPSS* commands in Figure 3.1 in a certain order, you should realize that there is a great deal of flexibility in how you actually order the commands. While you are learning how to use SPSS* and dealing with relatively straightforward procedures, you should insert the commands in the order listed in Figure 3.1 or follow the order suggested in the examples throughout the book. As you gain more confidence with SPSS*, however, you will see that different orders can be used to achieve desired goals. At the end of this chapter, we have listed some general guidelines and examples to help you think about how to order your commands.

DETAILED DESCRIPTION OF ADDITIONAL COMMANDS

Only those commands not described in Chapter 2 will be presented, and these will be presented in the order in which they appear in Figure 3.1.

In the descriptions of these commands, we will often refer to the example given in Chapter 2 (see Figure 2.10) involving a comparison of the effects of two drug levels (low and high) on three measures of activity in rats (SCORE1, SCORE2, and SCORE3).

MISSING VALUES Command

```
MISSING VALUES  SCORE1 (99) SCORE2 (9) SCORE3 (99)
```

Often, you are able to obtain complete data for all subjects or cases. Sometimes, however, subjects do not answer questions, information is not available, or equipment falters and you lose some data. If you do not wish to eliminate those cases or subjects entirely, you must give the computer a code for the missing data. Whatever code you choose for missing data, it cannot be a possible value of that variable. For example, if SCORE1 can range from 0 to 30 in our example, you could not use a value between 0 and 30 to represent missing data. A code such as 99 would work. Hence, in the preceding example, any SCORE1 given a code of 99 will be treated as missing data, any SCORE2 given a code of 9 will be treated as missing data, and any SCORE3 given a code of 99 will be treated as missing data.

In the more complicated example that follows, you can see some other methods of indicating missing values. Notice that the words LOWEST, THRU, and HIGHEST can be included within the parentheses and that variables having similar codes for missing values can be grouped

FIGURE 3.1 Commands in an SPSS^x File

NAME OF COMMAND	FUNCTION
TITLE	Provides a title for your printout.
DATA LIST	Tells the computer the names of your variables and the column locations for each variable. This command is required unless you are accessing an SPSS^x system file.
MISSING VALUES	Allows you to designate a code for missing data.
SET	Allows you to assign values to blank fields in your data set.
VARIABLE LABELS	Allows you to give more descriptive names to your variables. These will appear on the printout in addition to the abbreviated versions of the variable names in the DATA LIST command.
VALUE LABELS	Allows you to give descriptive labels to the different values or levels of your variables.
COMMENT	Enables you to place reminders and descriptions within your SPSS^x file.
RECODE	Allows you to change the codes or values of your variables.
COMPUTE	Allows you to perform computations on your data to create new variables.
IF	Specifies logical contingencies (e.g., greater than, equal to, less than) for creating new variables.
SELECT IF	Allows you to select certain cases or subjects for analysis and to eliminate others.
TEMPORARY	Specifies that data transformations (made with the RECODE, COMPUTE, IF, and SELECT IF commands) are temporary and apply only to the procedure that immediately follows the transformations.
LIST procedure	Causes a listing of your data to be printed.
Procedure command (e.g., ANOVA or PEARSON CORR)	Defines the particular statistical analysis to be performed.
OPTIONS	Specifies which, if any, of several choices are to be applied to the selected procedure. The available options are listed with the descriptions of the procedures.
STATISTICS	Specifies additional statistics to be performed along with the basic procedure. These choices are listed with the descriptions of the procedures.
BEGIN DATA	Tells the computer that the next line it reads is the first data line. This command must be used with the Within-File Method of reading data.
Data lines	Used in the Within-File Method of reading data. At least one line for each subject or case is presented here for the computer to read.
END DATA	Tells the computer that the last data line has been read. This command is required when using the Within-File Method of reading data.
FINISH	This is the last of the SPSS^x commands, and it indicates to the computer that the SPSS^x file is complete. This command is optional, but we suggest that you use it.

using the word TO. Also notice that three missing value codes are specified for variable Q12. This is the maximum number of missing value codes that can be specified for a particular variable. However, a larger range of missing values can be given with the keywords, LOWEST, THRU, and HIGHEST as shown for variables Q10 and Q11.

```
MISSING VALUES  EDUC (0) Q1 TO Q7 (9) Q10 (6 THRU HIGHEST)
                Q11 (LOWEST THRU 4) Q12 (1,7,9)
```

EDUC (0)

> Means that values of EDUC that are coded as 0 will be considered missing data.

Q1 TO Q7 (9)

> Means that a code of 9 for any of these seven variables will be considered missing data.

Q10 (6 THRU HIGHEST)

> Shows a slightly different approach. Here any value of RACE that is coded as 6 or higher (6, 7, 8, or 9) is considered missing data. Perhaps 6 means "don't know," 7 means "wasn't at home," and so on.

Q11 (LOWEST THRU 4)

> Shows the same approach using low numbers to code the different types of missing data. Maybe 1 means "did not wish to reveal," 2 means "not able to estimate," and so on.

Q12 (1,7,9)

> Means that values of Q12 that are coded as 1, 7, or 9 will be considered missing data.

There is one final shortcut. If all of your variables are scored similarly (e.g., on a 1 to 7 scale) and you wish to code missing data in the same way for all of them (e.g., with the value of 9), you could do the following:

```
MISSING VALUES ALL (9)
```

SET Command: Converting Blank Fields to Numeric Values

SPSS^x treats completely blank fields for numeric variables as missing values and not as zeros. (A *field* is the set of columns designated for that variable in the DATA LIST command.) Leading and ending blanks in a field are, in essence, considered to be zeros. Embedded blanks (i.e., blanks surrounded by numeric values), however, are treated as missing values. For example, consider the situation in which you specify (on your DATA LIST command) that VAR1 is to be read in columns 1 to 3. SPSS^x will interpret the following values for the cases listed as shown:

CASE	VALUES IN COLUMNS 1 TO 3	SPSS^x INTERPRETATION OF THE VALUES IN COLUMNS 1 TO 3
1	789	789
2	78	780
3	89	89
4	7 9	Missing value
5		Missing value

If you wish to have completely blank fields considered as zeros instead of missing values, you must use the SET command.

```
SET  BLANKS=0
```

This tells the computer to convert completely blank fields to zeros. Or, as follows, blank fields can be recoded into whatever value you desire.

```
SET  BLANKS=-99
```

VARIABLE LABELS Command

```
VARIABLE LABELS  DRUG "DOSAGE LEVEL" SCORE1 "ACTIVITY WHEEL RATE"
                 SCORE2 "FREERUN RATE" SCORE3 "T MAZE RATE"
```

An optional command, this allows you to have any or all of your variables identified more fully on the printout. First, you give the name of the variable exactly as it appears on the DATA LIST command, and you follow this with the fuller description. This is often quite useful in helping you reexamine your printouts later. Note that

1. A space appears between the variable name and the fuller description.
2. The fuller description may be a *maximum* of 40 columns. (On some computers, it may be as long as 120 characters.)
3. The fuller description must be enclosed within quotation marks (or apostrophes).

Although the preceding format for the VARIABLE LABELS command is entirely appropriate, variations on this format are possible. For example, to make your file easier to read, you may want to type the labels for each variable on separate lines. This method is shown as follows.

```
VARIABLE LABELS  DRUG "DOSAGE LEVEL"
                 SCORE1 "ACTIVITY WHEEL RATE"
                 SCORE2 "FREERUN RATE"
                 SCORE3 "T MAZE RATE"
```

VALUE LABELS Command

```
VALUE LABLES  DRUG 1 "HIGH DOSAGE" 2 "LOW DOSAGE"
```

Also optional, this command enables you to give a fuller printout label to the different levels of the variables or the different response categories. In our example, it would be useful only to specify levels of the independent variable—drug dosage. We have done so by enclosing the labels within quotation marks (apostrophes can be used instead of quotation marks) after the appropriate levels (1 and 2) of the DRUG variable. The activity scores, being continuous variables, cannot be broken down into categories for convenient labeling. The following example contains more than one variable.

```
VALUE LABELS  AGE 1 "UNDER 20" 2 "20-40" 3 "OVER 40"/Q1 TO Q10
              1 "STRONGLY DISAGREE" 2 "DISAGREE" 3 "NEUTRAL"
              4 "AGREE" 5 "STRONGLY AGREE"
```

Note that

1. Slashes separate variables.
2. The descriptions cannot occupy more than 20 columns. (On some computers, you can use as many as 60 columns.)

AGE is coded into three levels, and the labels are shown for each level. Similarly, variables Q1 to Q10 are coded into five response categories with appropriate labels. The word TO may be used to request identical labels for a set of variables. In the preceding example, Q1 TO Q10 will cause the computer to create the same labels for variables Q1, Q10, and all the variables that appeared between Q1 and Q10 on the DATA LIST command. Again, use labels only for those variables coded into discrete categories. Other variables (i.e., continuous variables) should not be labeled with this command.

Within the restrictions listed previously, the format for the VALUE LABELS command can vary. For example, you may want to start a new line for each variable (or groups of variables). This format is shown as follows.

```
VALUE LABELS  AGE 1 "UNDER 20" 2 "20-40" 3 "OVER 40"/
              Q1 TO Q10 1 "STRONGLY DISAGREE" 2 "DISAGREE"
              3 "NEUTRAL" 4 "AGREE" 5 "STRONGLY AGREE"
```

COMMENT Command

```
COMMENT  description
```

COMMENT commands enable you to place reminders and detailed descriptions within your SPSS^x file. Your entire SPSS^x file appears on your printout; thus the comment statements will enhance the readability or comprehension of your file and your printout by you and others. Other than appearing on your printout, COMMENT commands do not affect the processing of your program.

As an example, you may wish to remind yourself that file ACTDATA contains the drug data from female rats. In this case, you might type one of the following COMMENTS somewhere within your SPSS^x file.

```
COMMENT  FILE ACTDATA CONTAINS DRUG DATA FOR FEMALES
```

or

```
COMMENT  FILE ACTDATA CONTAINS DRUG DATA FOR FEMALE RATS FROM LITTERS
         1,2,3, AND 4
```

You might also want to describe the functions of several lines in your program. For example

```
COMMENT  THE NEXT TWO STATEMENTS CAUSE MALES OVER 30 TO BE SELECTED FOR
         THE ANALYSIS
```

You can also include comments immediately after the specifications in other commands. To do this, simply type the command as you normally would and then enclose your comment within the symbols /* and */. For example

```
MISSING VALUES  EDUC (0) /*ONLY NON-ZERO SCORES INCLUDED*/
```

or

```
COMPUTE  SUM=SCORE1+SCORE2 /*VARIABLE SUM REPRESENTS THE ADDITION OF
         SCORE1 AND SCORE2*/
```

RECODE Command

```
RECODE  SCORE1 (LOWEST THRU 5=1) (6 THRU 10=2) (11 THRU 20=3) (21 THRU
        HIGHEST=4)/
        SCORE2 (0 THRU 3.9=1) (ELSE=2)/
        SCORE3 (LOWEST THRU 9.99=1) (10 THRU HIGHEST=2)/
        SCORE4 TO SCORE7 (1,3,5=1) (ELSE=2)
```

This command allows you to make changes in variables—rename, cluster, and so forth. For convenience, the words LOWEST, HIGHEST, THRU, and ELSE may be used to group scores that will have the same recoded value. You may also list the variables to be given the same recoded value, separating them with commas. In our example, we might wish to cluster the activity scores into more discrete categories for a different type of analysis. Thus, for SCORE1, scores ranging from the lowest to a value of 5 will be recoded to a value of 1. Similarly, scores for SCORE1 ranging from 6 through 10 will be reassigned a value of 2, and so on. For SCORE2, scores from 0 to 3.9 will be reassigned the value of 1, and all other scores will be given the value of 2. The word TO may also be used to recode variables that have identical values. The last line in the example recodes variables SCORE4, SCORE7, and all the variables between SCORE4 and

SCORE7 on the DATA LIST statement. For all these variables, values of 1, 3, and 5 will be recoded as 1 and all other values will be assigned the value of 2.

Another common use of the RECODE command is to change alphabetically coded variables into numeric variables. For example, if we had kept a record of subjects' sex in our drug study using the codes M and F, we might want to convert these letters to numeric values for a statistical comparison.

```
RECODE  SEX ('M'=1) ('F'=2)
```

Note that the alphabetic characters are contained within apostrophes.

In analyzing the syntax of the RECODE command, you should be aware of two characteristics:

1. Each recoding expression must be enclosed within parentheses.
2. You may recode several variables with one RECODE command, but different variables must be separated with a slash:

```
RECODE  SEX ('M'=1) ('F'=2)/GROUP ('A'=1) ('B'=2) ('C'=3)
```

COMPUTE Command

```
COMPUTE  SUM=SCORE1+SCORE2+SCORE3
COMPUTE  MEANACT=(SCORE1+SCORE2+SCORE3)/3
```

A variety of computations may be used to transform your existing data for different kinds of analyses. The COMPUTE command allows you to generate new variables by arithmetic operations on other variables. The new variables can then be used in analyses that follow the COMPUTE command(s). Here we have created two new variables: a variable called SUM, which is the sum total of the three scores, and a variable called MEANACT, which is the mean of all three scores. Notice that each new variable must have a separate line and COMPUTE command. The COMPUTE command is very useful for scoring questionnaires, creating scales or indexes, and so forth.

The following list of COMPUTE commands demonstrates some of the different computations available. Obviously, they may be combined and weighted with numeric constants to fit mathematic formulas.

Addition	`COMPUTE  NEWVAR=VAR1+VAR2`
Subtraction	`COMPUTE  NEWVAR=VAR1-VAR2`
Multiplication	`COMPUTE  NEWVAR=VAR1*VAR2`
Division	`COMPUTE  NEWVAR=VAR1/VAR2`

Squaring	COMPUTE NEWVAR=VAR1**2
Square root	COMPUTE NEWVAR=SQRT(VAR1)
Absolute value	COMPUTE NEWVAR=ABS(VAR1–VAR2)
Logarithm (Base 10)	COMPUTE NEWVAR=LG10(VAR1)

When using more than one arithmetic operation, you may want to use parentheses to indicate the order of the computations to be performed. You must know several rules when you have more than one mathematic operation to perform:

Performed first: Operations within parentheses ( )
Performed second: * / ** SQRT
Performed last: + –

In an expression, if two operations have the same priority, the left operation is performed first (left-to-right rule).

For example, if A = 2, B = 4, C = 10, then

COMPUTE Z=A–B+C	Z = 8
COMPUTE Z=A–(B+C)	Z = –12
COMPUTE Z=A+B*C	Z = 42
COMPUTE Z=A+(B*C)	Z = 42
COMPUTE Z=(A+B)*C	Z = 60
COMPUTE Z=A/B*C	Z = 5
COMPUTE Z=A/(B*C)	Z = .05
COMPUTE Z=(10+A) / (C–B)	Z = 2
COMPUTE Z=10+A/C–B	Z = 6.2

Other arithmetic and statistical operations are available with the COMPUTE command. They include sine, arcsine, variance, and standard deviation. If you are interested in exploring other operations, consult the *SPSS^x User's Guide*, under the index heading of COMPUTE.

IF Command

```
IF  (SCORE1+SCORE2 LE 15) NEWVAR=1
IF  ((SCORE1+SCORE2) GE 16 AND (SCORE1+SCORE2) LE 30) NEWVAR=2
IF  (SCORE1+SCORE2 GT 30) NEWVAR=3
```

This command combines features of COMPUTE and RECODE. It renames and recodes variables that meet the specified requirements of certain logical relationships. In this example, the new variable NEWVAR will be coded as 1 if the sum of the scores is less than or equal (LE) to the value of 15. NEWVAR will be given the value of 2 if the sum of the scores is greater than or equal (GE) to 16 and less than or equal (LE) to 30. If the sum of the scores is greater than (GT) 30, the new variable NEWVAR will be given the value of 3. The relational and logical expressions that can be used with the IF command are:

GE   Greater than or equal to
LE   Less than or equal to
GT   Greater than
LT   Less than
EQ   Equal
NE   Not equal
AND And
OR   Or

You should note the following features of the IF command:

1. The arithmetic operations described with the COMPUTE command can also be used with the IF command.
2. All relational and logical expressions (e.g., GT) must be preceded and followed by a blank.
3. You may need to use one or more sets of parentheses to clarify the logic of your operations. Make sure, however, that you include an equal number of left and right parentheses.
4. Each new expression must have a separate line and IF command.

SELECT IF Command

```
SELECT IF  (SCORE1 GE 5)
```

Using the same logical expressions described with the IF command, you may ask the computer to analyze only certain cases that meet the criteria listed and exclude others. In our example, only those cases in which SCORE1 was greater than or equal to 5 would be analyzed. You might use this optional command to look at certain subgroups of subjects (e.g., males or persons over 65 years old). Although parentheses are not necessary in all situations, we suggest that you enclose the entire expression in them.

The words AND, OR, and additional parentheses may be used to specify more complicated selection criteria. For example

```
SELECT IF  ((SCORE1 LT 5 OR SCORE1 GT 10) AND SCORE2 GT 1)
```

This command causes a case to be selected for analysis if SCORE1 is less than 5 *or* greater than 10 *and* if SCORE2 is greater than 1.

You may include several SELECT IF statements in your file. You should be careful, however, when using more than one SELECT IF command, because the effects of each command are permanent. That is, SE-LECT IF commands are active from the time they are encountered in the program to the end of the program. Thus, the following commands would cause only those cases or subjects with SEX equal to 1 to be selected for the first CONDESCRIPTIVE procedure and *no* subjects to be selected for the second CONDESCRIPTIVE procedure (because a subject's sex cannot be both 1 and 2).

```
SELECT IF  (SEX EQ 1)
CONDESCRIPTIVE  VAR1
SELECT IF  (SEX EQ 2)
CONDESCRIPTIVE  VAR1
```

If you do not want your selections (or other transformations) to be permanent, use the TEMPORARY command described in the next section.

TEMPORARY Command

```
TEMPORARY
```

Placing the command TEMPORARY in front of any of the data transformation or selection commands (RECODE, COMPUTE, IF, SELECT IF) signifies that the transformation applies only to the procedure immediately following it and *not* to all procedures in the program.

Assume that you want to calculate descriptive statistics for VAR1, first for the males in your survey, second for the females in your survey, and third for all the subjects in your survey. To do this, you should use the following commands:

```
TEMPORARY
SELECT IF   (SEX EQ 1)
CONDESCRIPTIVE  VAR1        (results for males only)
TEMPORARY
SELECT IF   (SEX EQ 2)
CONDESCRIPTIVE  VAR1        (results for females only)
CONDESCRIPTIVE  VAR1        (results for all subjects)
```

As another example, consider the different effects of the two sequences of commands that follow.

```
TEMPORARY
SELECT IF   (SEX EQ 1)
CONDESCRIPTIVE  VAR1
SELECT IF   (IQ GT 130)
CONDESCRIPTIVE  VAR2
```

> Only subjects having SEX equal to 1 (e.g. males) will be included in the computations on variable VAR1. All subjects (males and females) with IQs above 130 will be included in the computations on VAR2.

```
SELECT IF    (SEX EQ 1)
CONDESCRIPTIVE  VAR1
SELECT IF    (IQ GT 130)
CONDESCRIPTIVE  VAR2
```

Only subjects having SEX equal to 1 will be included in the computations on VAR1. Only subjects with SEX equal to 1 and IQs greater than 130 will be selected for the computations on VAR2.

LIST Procedure

```
LIST  VARIABLES=SCORE1 SCORE2
```

From time to time, you may find it helpful to get a printed listing of your data. This is quite useful for proofreading the data lines and for checking your construction of the DATA LIST command, especially if you have gotten an error message and suspect that the data do not comply with the specifications on the DATA LIST command. In the preceding example, the LIST command causes a listing of the values of variables SCORE1 and SCORE2 to be printed for all cases or subjects. As shown in Figure 3.2, the output from the LIST command is not simply a copy of the data lines. Rather, it is a listing of your data in terms of the formats designated in your DATA LIST command and transformation commands. Thus, this listing should facilitate your detection of errors, such as specifying the wrong columns for variables in the DATA LIST command or specifying incorrect operations in your COMPUTE command.

The word TO may be used to request a listing for a set of variables. In the following example, a listing will be generated for SCORE1, SCORE4, and all the variables between SCORE1 and SCORE4 on the DATA LIST command.

```
LIST  VARIABLES=SCORE1 TO SCORE4
```

FIGURE 3.2   Output from the LIST Procedure

```
PROGRAM TO DEMONSTRATE THE FUNCTION OF THE LIST COMMAND

SCORE1 SCORE2
    2    3.6
   14    2.4
   12     .5
    3     .1
    4    1.6
   16    2.6
   25    3.1
   13    4.2
   11    5.3
    9    1.4

NUMBER OF CASES READ =    10    NUMBER OF CASES LISTED =    10
```

To request a listing of all variable values, simply type the word LIST as follows:

```
LIST
```

You should note that the LIST statement is actually a *procedure,* and thus its location in the SPSS^x file is constrained by the general restrictions that apply to all procedures. These are described in the next section.

MULTIPLE PROCEDURES AND THEIR LOCATION IN THE SPSS^x FILE

The location of the procedure statement(s) in your SPSS^x file depends, in part, on the method you are using for reading your data. Within the constraints that follow, you should remember that variable transformations and selections (using the RECODE, COMPUTE, IF, and SELECT IF commands) must be placed *before* the procedure(s) to which they apply. Also remember that a transformation will affect all procedures unless it is preceded by a TEMPORARY command.

Within-File Method. One (but no more than one) procedure command can precede the BEGIN DATA command. You may request as many additional procedures as you wish after the END DATA command. As an example, you may initially request PEARSON CORR (preceding the BEGIN DATA command) and later (following the END DATA command) request ANOVA and/or CONDESCRIPTIVE and/or other procedures on the same data. This method is illustrated in Figure 3.3.

FIGURE 3.3   Requesting Multiple Procedures: Within-File Method

```
JOB...
EXEC SPSSX...              (JCL commands for your computer system)
TITLE  "EXAMPLE OF MULTIPLE PROCEDURES"
DATA LIST  /VAR1 1 VAR2 3-4 VAR3 6-7
PEARSON CORR  VAR2 WITH VAR3
BEGIN DATA
 1 23 64
 1 91 87
 .
 .
 .
END DATA
ANOVA  VAR2 BY VAR1 (1,4)
CONDESCRIPTIVE  VAR2 VAR3
FINISH
END OF JOB...             (JCL command for your computer system)
```

Separate-File Method. With this method, you can request as many procedures as you desire after you have defined the data set (with the FILE HANDLE and DATA LIST or GET commands). This will be illustrated in the next section.

FILES AND FILE COMMUNICATION COMMANDS

SPSS[x] allows you to use a variety of methods for accessing data and performing statistical procedures. In most situations, you will probably type your SPSS[x] commands and your data lines in the same file (i.e., using the Within-File Method). Sometimes, however, you may find it helpful to use two or more files to accomplish your statistical goals. For example, you may want to type your SPSS[x] commands in one file and your data lines in another. Or you may want to create what is called an SPSS[x] system file and later access this file for additional analyses. Each of these latter two methods requires that you include in your file information that allows you to communicate with other files. The connection between files is accomplished with the file communication commands listed in Figure 3.4. (These commands are also reproduced on the last page of this manual.)

Before we describe the format and function of each file communication command, it will be helpful to clarify and expand on the concept of files. In general, a file is a set of commands and/or data lines that you create and store. In the following list we have described several different types of files with the names we have chosen to give them. We will refer to these different types of files as we explore the uses of the file communication commands.

1. *SPSS[x] file*: In this type of file, all of the information necessary for running an SPSS[x] program is included (i.e., JCL commands, SPSS[x] commands, and data lines). We described and used this type of file in Chapter 2 under the topic of Within-File Method of data entry. We have continued to use it throughout

FIGURE 3.4   File Communication Commands

NAME OF COMMAND	FUNCTION
FILE HANDLE	Provides a brief name for files that are to be stored or accessed. This command is required whenever you want to read information from and/or create other files.
SAVE	Tells the computer to store the data in an SPSS[x] system file for future use. This file can later be retrieved with the GET command.
GET	Tells the computer to access an SPSS[x] system file. Once the file is accessed, you can request statistical analyses without retyping the data lines and control commands.

the book, because it is the simplest and most straightforward approach to learning the logic of SPSS^x.

2. *SPSS^x command file*: This type of file contains only the JCL and SPSS^x commands—with data to be read from either a separate data file or an SPSS^x system file (both are described subsequently).

3. *Data file*: Only data lines are contained in this type of file. SPSS^x command files and data files were referred to in the discussion of the Separate-File Method of data entry in Chapter 2. We will show you how to link these two types of files with the FILE HANDLE command.

4. *SPSS^x system file*: This type of file contains the data and information about the data (i.e., descriptive information and transformations created with the DATA LIST, VARIABLE LABELS, VALUE LABELS, MISSING VALUES, COMPUTE, IF, SELECT IF, and RECODE commands). This information is stored (with the SAVE command) in a special format for efficient accessing and processing by the SPSS^x system. This allows the user to run subsequent analyses at future times on the same data set with a minimum number of SPSS^x commands. We will show you how the FILE HANDLE command enables you to store (SAVE) and access (GET) this type of file.

FILE HANDLE Command

```
FILE HANDLE  ACTDATA/local system specifications
```

As described earlier, there may be situations in which you want to communicate between files. In these situations, you must identify the name, or "handle," of each file that you are accessing and/or creating, and you do this with the FILE HANDLE command. Basically, then, a FILE HANDLE command is needed in your program whenever you want to read information from another file and/or create (write to) a new file.

In the preceding example, the name of the file is ACTDATA. The file name *cannot be longer than eight characters, and the first character must be alphabetic*. The remaining characters can be alphabetic and/or numeric (e.g., ACTIV1 and AC9999 are valid file names). In addition, no blanks can be inserted within the file name (e.g., ACT 1 and ACT DATA are invalid file names). If you are using several files, each file must have a unique name and a separate FILE HANDLE command. After a name is provided for the file with the FILE HANDLE command, a slash (/) followed by some additional specifications for your local computer system may be necessary. The local system specifications vary for different computer systems (as is the case for the Job Control Language described in Chapter 2). (Note: On some computers, the actual FILE HANDLE command is not used, but the name of the file must be specified in the JCL commands.) To find out what additional specifications are required for your computer, either ask for information from the personnel in your computer center or request this information by using the keyword LOCAL on the INFO command described in Chapter 14. When you discover the FILE HANDLE (or in some cases, JCL) specifications that are necessary for

FIGURE 3.9   An Example Using the GET Command to Access a System File

```
JOB...
EXEC SPSSX...              (JCL commands for your computer system)
TITLE  "EXAMPLE OF SYSTEM FILE RETRIEVAL"
FILE HANDLE  SFACT/local system specifications
GET  FILE=SFACT
T-TEST  GROUPS=DRUG/VARIABLES=SCORE1 TO SCORE3
OPTIONS  2
FINISH
END OF JOB...            (JCL command for your computer system)
```

```
FILE HANDLE  SFACT/local system specifications
GET  FILE=SFACT
```

As shown, the name of the file that you wish to access must appear in the FILE HANDLE command and in the GET command after the keyword FILE=. In the example shown in Figure 3.9, the GET command will cause the computer to find the file called SFACT, which was stored earlier with a SAVE command. A T-TEST procedure would then be performed on the data that were stored in file SFACT. As you can see, this is an extremely efficient way of performing further analyses on your data. Note again that the data in SFACT have already been defined, and therefore further definitions of the data (e.g., with the DATA LIST command) are not needed. You may include more than one procedure command after the GET FILE statement, as shown in Figure 3.10.

In some cases, you may want to use the Separate-File Method of reading data and also to save your data in a system file. This situation requires that you communicate with two different files and use two FILE HANDLE commands. For example, if you want to read your data from the data file ACTDATA and later store those same data in system file SFACT,

FIGURE 3.10   Multiple Procedures with GET Command

```
JOB...
EXEC SPSSX...              (JCL commands for your computer system)
TITLE  "EXAMPLE OF SYSTEM FILE RETRIEVAL"
FILE HANDLE  SFACT/local system specifications
GET  FILE=SFACT
T-TEST  GROUPS=DRUG/VARIABLES=SCORE1 TO SCORE3
OPTIONS  2
PEARSON CORR  SCORE1 TO SCORE3
CONDESCRIPTIVE  SCORE1 TO SCORE3
FINISH
END OF JOB...            (JCL command for your computer system)
```

FIGURE 3.11   Illustration of a Program that Reads Data from a Separate File and Stores the Data in an SPSS^x System File

```
JOB. . .
EXEC SPSSX. . .                (JCL commands for your computer system)
TITLE  "SPSSX SYSTEM FILE WITH SEPARATE DATA FILE"
FILE HANDLE  ACTDATA/local system specifications
FILE HANDLE  SFACT/local system specifications
DATA LIST  FILE=ACTDATA/DRUG 1 SCORE1 2-3 SCORE2 4-6 SCORE3 7-11
(Procedure)
SAVE  OUTFILE=SFACT
FINISH
END OF JOB. . .               (JCL command for your computer system)
```

then you would use two FILE HANDLE commands as shown in Figure 3.11. Notice that a different name must be indicated on each FILE HANDLE command.

ORDER OF SPSS^x COMMANDS

Basically, you should use your knowledge of the logic of SPSS^x to determine the order of commands. *In effect, most SPSS^x commands are executed in the order in which they occur in the file, and this imposes certain restrictions on your ordering of commands.* Thus, you need to define a file (with the FILE HANDLE command) before you can read from the file (with the DATA LIST or GET commands) or store the file (with the SAVE command). Similarly, you must define your variables and tell the computer where to read them (with the DATA LIST command) before you can create labels for these variables (with the VARIABLE LABELS and VALUE LABELS commands), transform the variables (e.g., with the RECODE command), or execute a procedure on these variables (e.g., with the CONDESCRIPTIVE command). To illustrate, assume that you wish to create a new variable called X2 (using the COMPUTE command) and to give this variable a label (with the VARIABLE LABELS command). In this case, you should put the VARIABLE LABELS command for the new variable after the COMPUTE command. You should also realize that you can insert a command in several locations. For example, you can have a VARIABLE LABELS command after the DATA LIST command and another one after the COMPUTE command.

Several additional restrictions follow:

1. The STATISTICS and OPTIONS commands must immediately follow the procedure to which they refer.
2. SPSS^x commands cannot be inserted *within* the set of data lines. Further,

FIGURE 3.12 Data Sheet for the Teaching-Methods Experiment

SUBJECT NO.	TEACHING METHOD[a]	YEAR IN COLLEGE[b]	SAT VERBAL	SAT MATH	AGE	TEST 1	TEST 2	TEST 3	TEST 4	TEST 5	TEST 6	FINAL EXAM
01	1	1	400	720	18.6	66	82	74	82	88	80	78
02	1	1	450	450	17.9	76	86	80	86	88	-99	85
03	1	2	470	500	19.4	74	80	90	94	96	94	92
04	1	2	450	470	21.0	-99	78	82	80	96	96	94
05	1	3	520	500	20.7	54	62	76	80	64	72	80
06	1	3	750	800	20.3	92	86	96	90	93	92	89
07	1	4	700	620	21.8	98	100	100	98	98	76	95
08	1	4	670	670	24.3	88	92	96	90	90	95	85
09	2	1	600	560	36.0	70	84	80	72	76	84	75
10	2	1	425	500	18.2	87	78	64	54	64	67	-99
11	2	2	670	580	19.9	60	62	76	86	74	74	88
12	2	2	680	720	19.6	84	96	92	-99	93	94	95
13	2	3	500	650	20.8	91	81	77	93	89	86	89
14	2	3	470	450	21.0	52	68	64	65	77	59	54
15	2	4	720	520	23.1	84	74	82	83	80	83	87
16	2	4	500	500	22.7	74	76	74	77	77	83	62

[a]Code for teaching method: lecture = 1, programmed = 2.
[b]Code for year in college: freshman = 1, sophomore = 2, junior = 3, senior = 4.

when using the Within-File Method of reading data, you cannot include any commands between the BEGIN DATA and END DATA commands.

3. As noted, you must define your data (with the DATA LIST command) before you use any subsequent commands involving these variables (e.g., procedure commands, VARIABLE LABELS, VALUE LABELS, RECODE, COMPUTE).

4. As described earlier, when the Within-File Method of reading data is used, only one procedure command can precede the BEGIN DATA command. Additional procedures can be requested after the END DATA command.

COMPLETE EXAMPLE USING ADDITIONAL SPSSˣ COMMANDS: TEACHING-METHODS EXPERIMENT

Suppose that in an experiment the traditional lecture method of learning was contrasted with the self-paced method. Subjects were tested individually and either exposed to a videotaped lecture or allowed to work on the same material using a computer programmed for individual rates of learning. Several sessions were run throughout the term, resulting in six test scores plus a final examination score. Other data collected included year in college, verbal and math SAT scores, and age. The data sheet appears in Figure 3.12, the SPSSˣ file in Figure 3.13, and the functions of some of the commands in Figure 3.14.

ADDITIONAL ANALYSES USING AN SPSSˣ SYSTEM FILE

If the data are saved in TCHFILE, then the GET command can be used to perform additional analyses. For example, the program listed in Figure 3.15 would cause the computer to compute the correlation between verbal SAT scores (VERB) and math SAT scores (MATH).

FIGURE 3.13   SPSSˣ File for the Teaching-Methods Experiment

```
JOB...
EXEC SPSSX...                (JCL commands for your computer system)
TITLE   "TEACHING METHODS EXPERIMENT"
FILE HANDLE    TCHFILE/local system specifications
COMMENT    ***SYSTEM FILE CONTAINING THE DATA WILL BE NAMED TCHFILE
DATA LIST    /SNUM 1-2 METH 4 YEAR 6 VERB 8-10 MATH 12-14 AGE 16-19
             TEST1 TO TEST6 21-43 FINAL 45-47
MISSING VALUES    TEST1 TO FINAL (-99)
VARIABLE LABELS    METH "METHOD OF TEACHING"
                   YEAR "YEAR IN COLLEGE"
                   VERB "VERBAL SAT SCORE"
                   MATH "MATH SAT SCORE"
```

continued

FIGURE 3.13 *(Continued)*

```
                    AGE "CHRONOLOGICAL AGE IN YEARS"
                    TEST1 "PERFORMANCE ON FIRST TEST"
                    TEST2 "PERFORMANCE ON SECOND TEST"
                    TEST3 "PERFORMANCE ON THIRD TEST"
                    TEST4 "PERFORMANCE ON FOURTH TEST"
                    TEST5 "PERFORMANCE ON FIFTH TEST"
                    TEST6 "PERFORMANCE ON SIXTH TEST"
                    FINAL "PERFORMANCE ON FINAL EXAM"
VALUE LABELS    METH 1 "LECTURE METHOD" 2 "DISCUSSION METHOD"/
                YEAR 1 "FRESHMAN" 2 "SOPHOMORE" 3 "JUNIOR"
                4 "SENIOR"
SELECT IF    (VERB GT 300 AND VERB LT 750)
RECODE    YEAR (2 THRU 4=2)
COMPUTE   SATTOT=VERB+MATH
COMPUTE   TERMTOT=TEST1+TEST2+TEST3+TEST4+TEST5+TEST6+FINAL
COMPUTE   ADJTOT=TEST1+TEST2+TEST3+TEST4+TEST5+TEST6+(3*FINAL)
COMMENT   ***ADDITIONAL VARIABLE LABELS WILL BE INCLUDED FOR THE
          COMPUTED VARIABLES--SATTOT, TERMTOT, AND ADJTOT
VARIABLE LABELS    SATTOT "TOTAL SAT SCORE"
                   TERMTOT "SUM OF ALL TESTS OVER TERM"
                   ADJTOT "TERM TOTAL WITH FINAL COUNTING 3 TESTS"
PEARSON CORR   TERMTOT WITH SATTOT
STATISTICS    1
BEGIN DATA
01 1 1 400 720 18.6  66  82  74  82  88  80  78
02 1 1 450 450 17.9  76  86  80  86  88 -99  85
03 1 2 470 500 19.4  74  80  90  94  96  94  92
04 1 2 450 470 21.0 -99  78  82  80  96  96  94
05 1 3 520 500 20.7  54  62  76  80  64  72  80
06 1 3 750 800 20.3  92  86  96  90  93  92  89
07 1 4 700 620 21.8  98 100 100  98  98  76  95
08 1 4 670 670 24.3  88  92  96  90  90  95  85
09 2 1 600 560 36.0  70  84  80  72  76  84  75
10 2 1 425 500 18.2  87  78  64  54  64  67 -99
11 2 2 670 580 19.9  60  62  76  86  74  74  88
12 2 2 680 720 19.6  84  96  92 -99  93  94  95
13 2 3 500 650 20.8  91  81  77  93  89  86  89
14 2 3 470 450 21.0  52  68  64  65  77  59  54
15 2 4 720 520 23.1  84  74  82  83  80  83  87
16 2 4 500 500 22.7  74  76  74  77  77  83  62
END DATA
T-TEST    GROUPS=YEAR/VARIABLES=ADJTOT
SAVE    OUTFILE=TCHFILE
FINISH
END OF JOB...            (JCL command for your computer system)
```

FIGURE 3.14   Functions of Some Commands in the SPSS^x File for the Teaching-Methods Experiment

---

MISSING VALUES   TEST1 TO FINAL (-99)

        Causes all scores that are equal to −99 for variables TEST1, TEST2, TEST3, TEST4, TEST5, TEST6, and FINAL to be treated as missing data. Notice that −99 is a good code for missing values in this example because it is not a possible test score.

SELECT IF   (VERB GT 300 AND VERB LT 750)

        Causes only the cases that have verbal scores between 300 and 750 to be included in the analyses. In effect, this statement causes the extreme verbal SAT scores to be excluded from all subsequent analyses.

RECODE   YEAR (2 THRU 4=2)

        Recodes all sophomores, juniors, and seniors into the same group. This command would enable you to compare freshmen to all upperclassmen (without distinguishing between sophomores, juniors, and seniors).

COMPUTE   SATTOT=VERB+MATH

        Creates a new variable called SATTOT, which represents the combined verbal and math scores.

VARIABLE LABELS   SATTOT "TOTAL SAT SCORE"

        Creates a label for variable SATTOT, which will appear on your printout, thereby helping you identify the variable. Note that the label for SATTOT must appear after the COMPUTE command (which is the command that created the variable). Variables need to be defined before they can be labeled.

PEARSON CORR   TERMTOT WITH SATTOT

        Causes the Pearson product-moment correlation coefficient to be computed between TERMTOT and SATTOT. (This procedure is described in Chapter 11.)

STATISTICS   1

        Causes the mean and standard deviation to be printed out for TERMTOT and SATTOT. It is a choice available with the PEARSON CORR procedure.

T-TEST   GROUPS=YEAR/VARIABLES=ADJTOT

        Causes the computer to test for a significant difference between the mean adjusted total scores (ADJTOT) of freshmen and upperclassmen. Note that the second procedure command occurs after the data. (The T-TEST procedure is described in Chapters 7 and 8.) Also note that the earlier SELECT IF command applies to this procedure as well. Thus only

---

continued

FIGURE 3.14   *(Continued)*

freshmen and upperclassmen with verbal SAT scores between 300 and 750 will be included in the T-TEST procedure. If you wished to have the SELECT IF statement apply only to the PEARSON CORR procedure and not to the T-TEST procedure, then you could have typed a TEMPORARY command immediately before the SELECT IF command.

SAVE OUTFILE=TCHFILE

This, along with the FILE HANDLE command, causes the data to be saved in an SPSS^x system file called TCHFILE. Note that the program would compute the identical statistics without the FILE HANDLE and SAVE commands. Thus you do not have to include them unless you intend to perform further analyses.

FIGURE 3.15   SPSS^x File Using the GET Command to Access System File TCHFILE

```
JOB...
EXEC SPSSX...          (JCL commands for your computer system)
TITLE  "CORRELATION OF VERBAL SAT AND MATH SAT"
FILE HANDLE TCHFILE/local system specifications
GET  FILE=TCHFILE
PEARSON CORR  VERB WITH MATH
STATISTICS  1
FINISH
END OF JOB...          (JCL command for your computer system)
```

CONDESCRIPTIVE:
Descriptive Statistics

PURPOSE

CONDESCRIPTIVE is the SPSS^x procedure that computes descriptive statistics. These statistics are used to summarize a set of scores in a convenient form and typically are the first calculations performed on a distribution of scores. With the CONDESCRIPTIVE procedure, any or all of the following statistics can be calculated: mean, variance, standard deviation, sum of the scores, minimum and maximum scores, range, standard error of the mean, skewness, and kurtosis.

GENERAL FORMAT AND VARIATIONS OF THE CONDESCRIPTIVE COMMAND

After typing the command CONDESCRIPTIVE, you should type the name of the variable for which you wish to have descriptive statistics calculated. Remember, the variable name must be spelled exactly as it appears in the DATA LIST command:

```
CONDESCRIPTIVE VARA
```

To compute statistics for several variables, the variable names can be listed (separated by at least one space) as shown:

```
CONDESCRIPTIVE VARA VARB VARC VARD
```

or the word TO can be placed between variable names:

```
CONDESCRIPTIVE VARA TO VARD
```

Note the function of the word TO in the preceding example. Using the word TO between these two variables causes descriptive statistics to be computed for VARA, VARD, and all of the variables that appeared between VARA and VARD on the DATA LIST command.

Both forms of specifying variables may be used in the same CONDE-SCRIPTIVE command. Thus, the format used in the following example is also appropriate:

```
CONDESCRIPTIVE VARA TO VARD VARL VART
```

One final method of listing variables is to use the word ALL. Thus, if you would like to compute descriptive statistics for all the variables in your DATA LIST statement, as well as all of the variables that you have created (e.g., with a COMPUTE statement), use the following format:

```
CONDESCRIPTIVE ALL
```

COMMONLY USED OPTIONS

Seven OPTIONS are available with the CONDESCRIPTIVE procedure. The OPTIONS command, if used, follows the CONDESCRIPTIVE statement. You may use some or none of these options in your program. Five of the more frequently used are described subsequently, and the others can be found in the CONDESCRIPTIVE chapter of the *SPSS* *User's Guide*. To cause an option to be executed, type the word OPTIONS beginning in column 1, skip at least one space, and then type the desired option number.

```
OPTIONS 1
```

> Causes all MISSING VALUES designations to be ignored. Hence, all data would be included in the calculation of the descriptive statistics—even that with codes representing missing data.

```
OPTIONS 5
```

> Causes a case to be eliminated from all statistical computations if that case contains missing data on *any* of the variables listed on the CONDESCRPTIVE command. If these two options are not used, a subject or case is excluded only from those analyses involving the missing score.

OPTIONS 4

> Causes tables to be printed that contain the variable names and
> the page numbers of the printout where the computed statistics
> for those variables can be found. This option is useful for
> locating specific analyses when you have many pages of output.
> Two tables will be printed, and these will appear at the end of
> the CONDESCRIPTIVE output. In one table, the variables are
> listed alphabetically, and in the other, the variables are listed
> according to their position in the CONDESCRIPTIVE
> statement.

OPTIONS 6

> This option affects the printout of your statistics. With this
> option, the computer first prints the name of a variable and
> then lists the statistics below the variable name. The computer
> then goes on to use the same format for the next variable.
> OPTIONS 6 has the effect of separating your variables on the
> printout. If this option is not used, the default format for
> printing the requested statistics will be in effect. That is, the
> requested statistics for the different variables are listed in
> columns (see Figure 4.6).

OPTIONS 7

> Causes the computer to print the results within 80 columns.

To invoke several options, use only one OPTIONS command and
then list the numbers of the appropriate options (separated by at least one
space). For example

OPTIONS 1 4

You may omit the OPTIONS command altogether if you do not wish
to use any of the possible options.

STATISTICS AVAILABLE WITH CONDESCRIPTIVE

You may select any or all of the 10 STATISTICS available with CONDE-
SCRIPTIVE. Each statistic is associated with a particular number, and the
reference numbers for the available STATISTICS are shown in Figure 4.1.
Note that the numbers 3 and 4 are not associated with any particular
statistic and should not be used.
To access a particular statistical procedure, you would use the following format:

STATISTICS   (number of the statistic that you wish)

FIGURE 4.1   Reference Numbers for CONDESCRIPTIVE STATISTICS

NUMBER	STATISTIC
1	Mean
2	Standard error of the mean
5	Standard deviation
6	Variance
7	Kurtosis
8	Skewness
9	Range
10	Minimum score—lowest score in distribution
11	Maximum score—highest score in distribution
12	Sum of the scores
13	Mean, standard deviation, minimum score, and maximum score

For example

STATISTICS   1   (to have the mean computed)

or

STATISTICS   8   (to have skewness computed)

To compute several statistics, simply list the appropriate numbers on the same line and separate them by at least one space. For example, to calculate the mean, standard deviation, variance, and range, the following format is appropriate:

STATISTICS   1 5 6 9

If you wish to calculate the mean, standard deviation, minimum score, and maximum score, you can either list the four appropriate numbers or use the number 13:

STATISTICS   13

If you also wish to compute skewness, then you may use the following form:

STATISTICS   8 13

To have all of the statistics calculated, simply type the word ALL:

STATISTICS   ALL

As described in Chapter 2, the STATISTICS command follows the OPTIONS command. If no OPTIONS are selected, then the STATIS-TICS statement should follow the CONDESCRIPTIVE command. If you do not include a STATISTICS command, the mean, standard deviation,

FIGURE 4.2   Data Sheet for Nursing Home Study

RESPONDENT	AGE	PERSONALITY SCORE	MEDICAL INDEX	ACTIVITY SCORE
01	76	78	65	4.7
02	83	67	43	−2.7
03	68	88	100	−1.4
04	94	59	76	.3
05	77	100	91	4.3
.	.	.	.	.
.	.	.	.	.
.	.	.	.	.
96	36	62	74	3.8

minimum score, and maximum score will be calculated and printed in your printout as if you had specified STATISTICS 13 or STATISTICS 1 5 10 11.

PUTTING THE SPSSˣ FILE TOGETHER

At this point, you should try to write an SPSSˣ file that will calculate descriptive statistics for several variables. Use the following information to write your SPSSˣ file.

For future planning purposes, assume that you are interested in developing a profile of nursing home users in a particular county. To do this, you collected the following information from a random sample of 96 current nursing home residents:

1. Age (The oldest person was 94 years old.)
2. A personality test score indicating mental health (This score ranges from 0 to 100.)
3. A medical index of physical health (This score ranges from 0 to 100.)
4. A daily activity score (This score ranges from −5.0 to +5.0.)

The format of the data sheet from this survey is shown in Figure 4.2. Try to write an SPSSˣ file that computes all 10 descriptive statistics for each of the four variables. Then check what you have written with the SPSSˣ file that appears in Figure 4.3.

Notes and Variations

```
DATA LIST   /AGE 4-5 PERSCOR 7-9 MEDSCOR 11-13 ACTSCOR 15-18
```
Although the variables and columns on the DATA LIST command are appropriate for the positions of the variables in the data lines, you should realize that there are alternative forms of typing in your data. For example, you could have

reduced the number of typing strokes in your data lines by omitting the respondent identification numbers, the blank spaces between the variables, and the decimal points for the variable ACTSCOR. Thus, if the data lines were typed in the following format

```
(Columns 1.........11)
        ↓         ↓
       76 78 65  47
       83 67 43-27
       68 88100-14
       94 59 76   3
       77100 91  43
           .
           .
           .
       36 62 74  38
```

The DATA LIST statement should look like the following:

```
DATA LIST   /AGE 1-2 PERSCOR 3-5 MEDSCOR 6-8
             ACTSCOR 9-11 (1)
```

Recall that the (1) after ACTSCOR 9-11 means that one decimal place is to be assumed.

FIGURE 4.3 SPSS^x File for Nursing Home Study

```
JOB...
EXEC SPSSX...              (JCL commands for your computer system)
TITLE   "NURSING HOME STUDY"
DATA LIST   /AGE 4-5 PERSCOR 7-9 MEDSCOR 11-13 ACTSCOR 15-18
VARIABLE LABELS   AGE "AGE OF RESIDENTS"
                  PERSCOR "PERSONALITY SCORE"
                  MEDSCOR "MEDICAL INDEX OF PHYSICAL HEALTH"
                  ACTSCOR "DAILY ACTIVITY SCORE"
CONDESCRIPTIVE   AGE TO ACTSCOR
STATISTICS    ALL
BEGIN DATA
01 76   78   65    4.7
02 83   67   43  -2.7
03 68   88  100  -1.4
04 94   59   76    .3
05 77  100   91    4.3
 .
 .
 .
96 36   62   74    3.8
END DATA
FINISH
END OF JOB...            (JCL command for your computer system)
```

VARIABLE LABELS   AGE "AGE OF RESIDENTS"

> Causes a more extensive label of the variable (up to 40 columns) to appear on the printout. This is an optional command.

CONDESCRIPTIVE   AGE TO ACTSCOR

> Causes the computer to calculate descriptive statistics for all four variables (AGE, PERSCOR, MEDSCOR, ACTSCOR). The following command would cause the identical analyses to be performed:
>
> CONDESCRIPTIVE   AGE PERSCOR MEDSCOR ACTSCOR

STATISTICS   ALL

> This statement requests computation of all 10 statistics.

Note: The variables listed in the VARIABLE LABELS and CONDESCRIPTIVE commands must be spelled exactly as they appear in the DATA LIST statement.

The following examples should give you additional practice in writing SPSS˟ files. Also, the uses of the SAVE and GET commands are demonstrated, and sample printouts and explanations of these printouts are presented.

EXAMPLE 1: MARKETING SURVEY

Suppose that you wished to assess characteristics of customers of a particular fast food restaurant (Jack's). To do this, you developed a short questionnaire that required people to indicate:

1. Their age
2. Their annual family income (to the nearest thousand)
3. The number of people in their party
4. The number of meals that they have had at a restaurant this month
5. The number of meals that they have had at a fast food restaurant this month
6. The number of meals that they have had at Jack's this month

Every twentieth adult customer was given a questionnaire to fill out, and over a two-week period, 120 questionnaires were completed.

Initially, you want to compute the mean, standard deviation, range, and minimum and maximum scores for all six questions or variables. The data sheet for this study is presented in Figure 4.4, and an appropriate SPSS˟ file for performing CONDESCRIPTIVE is presented in Figure 4.5.

FIGURE 4.4 Data Sheet for Marketing Survey

RESPONDENT	AGE	INCOME	PARTY SIZE	NO. OF MEALS PER MONTH AT RESTAURANT	NO. OF MEALS PER MONTH AT FAST FOOD RESTAURANT	NO. OF MEALS PER MONTH AT JACK'S
001	24	12000	16	6	4	1
002	33	19500	2	25	24	12
003	60	38000	4	8	2	1
004	41	18000	3	16	7	4
005	55	26000	1	1	0	0
.	.	.	.	.	.	.
.	.	.	.	.	.	.
.	.	.	.	.	.	.
120	38	24000	2	12	8	2

FIGURE 4.5 SPSS× File for Marketing Survey

```
JOB...
EXEC SPSSX...                  (JCL commands for your computer system)
TITLE     "MARKETING SURVEY OF JACK'S RESTAURANT"
FILE HANDLE    JSURVEY/local system specifications
DATA LIST    /AGE 5-6 INCOME 8-12 PARTY 14-15 MEALR 17-18 MEALFF 20-21
             MEALJ 23-24
VARIABLE LABELS    AGE "AGE OF RESPONDENTS"
                   INCOME "INCOME OF RESPONDENTS"
                   PARTY "NUMBER IN PARTY"
                   MEALR "NUMBER MEALS AT A RESTAURANT"
                   MEALFF "NUMBER MEALS AT A FAST FOOD RESTAURANT"
                   MEALJ "NUMBER OF MEALS AT JACK'S"
CONDESCRIPTIVE     AGE TO MEALJ
STATISTICS    9 13
BEGIN DATA
001 24 12000 16  6  4  1
002 33 19500  2 25 24 12
003 60 38000  4  8  2  1
004 41 18000  3 16  7  4
005 55 26000  1  1  0  0
.
.
.
120 38 24000  2 12  8  2
END DATA
SAVE    OUTFILE=JSURVEY
FINISH
END OF JOB...                  (JCL command for your computer system)
```

FIGURE 4.6 Output for CONDESCRIPTIVE Procedure Applied to Marketing Survey

MARKETING SURVEY OF JACK'S RESTAURANT

NUMBER OF VALID OBSERVATIONS (LISTWISE) =   120.00

VARIABLE	MEAN	STD DEV	RANGE	MINIMUM	MAXIMUM	VALID N	LABEL
AGE	42.433	14.095	48.000	18.000	66.000	120	AGE OF RESPONDENTS
INCOME	23608.333	10352.035	58000.000	12000.000	70000.000	120	INCOME OF RESPONDENTS
PARTY	3.283	2.071	15.000	1.000	16.000	120	NUMBER IN PARTY
MEALR	11.358	8.538	24.000	1.000	25.000	120	NUMBER MEALS AT A RESTAURANT
MEALFF	7.567	8.778	24.000	.000	24.000	120	NUMBER MEALS AT A FAST-FOOD RESTAURANT
MEALJ	3.733	4.587	17.000	.000	17.000	120	NUMBER OF MEALS AT JACK'S

Output from the Marketing Survey

As shown in Figure 4.6, the output from the CONDESCRIPTIVE procedure is explicitly labeled. A separate column exists for each statistic requested, and the values of these statistics appear to the right of the appropriate variables. Also, note that the number of valid scores is listed at the top of the table (that is, the number of scores used in the calculations of the statistics, depending on the missing value or selection specifications in your file).

EXAMPLE 2: MARKETING SURVEY—ADDITIONAL ANALYSES

Assume that you now want to perform further analyses to determine the income levels and ages of low, medium, and heavy users of Jack's restaurant. In consultation with the owner of Jack's, you decide that the levels of use should be operationally defined as:

Low (zero or one meal per month)
Medium (two to five meals per month)
High (over five meals per month)

Hence, you first want to categorize the respondents or cases on the basis of the frequency of their usage of the restaurant. You can do this with the SELECT IF command. Then the desired statistics (in this case, means and standard deviations) would be computed for each of these subsets of cases.

FIGURE 4.7 **SPSS^x File of Additional Analyses on Marketing Survey**

```
JOB...
EXEC SPSSX...              (JCL commands for your computer system)
TITLE   "MARKETING SURVEY—ADDITIONAL ANALYSES"
FILE HANDLE    JSURVEY/local system specifications
GET    FILE=JSURVEY
TEMPORARY
SELECT IF    (MEALJ LE 1)
CONDESCRIPTIVE    AGE INCOME
STATISTICS    1 5
TEMPORARY
SELECT IF    (MEALJ GE 2 AND MEALJ LE 5)
CONDESCRIPTIVE    AGE INCOME
STATISTICS    1 5
SELECT IF    (MEALJ GE 6)
CONDESCRIPTIVE    AGE INCOME
STATISTICS    1 5
FINISH
END OF JOB...           (JCL command for your computer system)
```

FIGURE 4.8   Output for Additional Analyses on Marketing Survey

```
TEMPORARY
SELECT IF    (MEALJ LE 1)
CONDESCRIPTIVE    AGE INCOME
STATISTICS    1 5


NUMBER OF VALID OBSERVATIONS (LISTWISE) =          71.00

VARIABLE       MEAN      STD DEV VALID N   LABEL

AGE         46.127      16.249      71    AGE OF RESPONDENTS
INCOME   25323.944   10775.335      71    INCOME OF RESPONDENTS



TEMPORARY
SELECT IF    (MEALJ GE 2 AND MEALJ LE 5)
CONDESCRIPTIVE    AGE INCOME
STATISTICS    1 5


NUMBER OF VALID OBSERVATIONS (LISTWISE) =          24.00

VARIABLE       MEAN      STD DEV VALID N   LABEL

AGE         40.000       7.813      24    AGE OF RESPONDENTS
INCOME   20708.333    8487.736      24    INCOME OF RESPONDENTS



SELECT IF    (MEALJ GE 6)
CONDESCRIPTIVE    AGE INCOME
STATISTICS    1 5


NUMBER OF VALID OBSERVATIONS (LISTWISE) =          25.00

VARIABLE       MEAN      STD DEV VALID N   LABEL

AGE         34.280       6.400      25    AGE OF RESPONDENTS
INCOME   21520.000   10100.000      25    INCOME OF RESPONDENTS
```

Because the data from the initial analysis were saved in system file JSURVEY, the GET command can be used to run the additional analyses. The SPSS^x file is presented in Figure 4.7, and the output is shown in Figure 4.8. Note that the TEMPORARY command before the SELECT IF command causes that selection to apply only to the procedure that immediately follows it and not to other procedures.

LIMITATIONS OF CONDESCRIPTIVE

There is no maximum number of variables that can be listed on a single CONDESCRIPTIVE command. Although unlikely, it is possible that your requests will exceed the workspace limitations of your computer. If this occurs, SPSS^x will start performing the CONDESCRIPTIVE procedure for the variables listed and will stop when the limitation is exceeded. You should exclude the analyzed variables and then include the unanalyzed variables in a subsequent run of your program.

5

FREQUENCIES: One-Way Frequency Distributions and Related Statistics

PURPOSE

The FREQUENCIES procedure is used to find and graph the number of cases falling into different response categories for discrete (discontinuous) variables. For instance, in a sample of voters, one might determine the number or percentage of voters who favor each of the candidates in a given election. In addition, the procedure allows one to obtain the appropriate descriptive statistics (e.g., mean, median, mode, standard deviation) associated with the variables.

CHOOSING INTEGER VERSUS GENERAL MODES FOR THE FREQUENCIES PROCEDURE

There are two possible ways to set up the FREQUENCIES procedure. One is used if you have all response categories coded numerically. This is called the *integer mode*. If, on the other hand, some of your response categories have alphabetic codes (e.g., codes of M and F for subject sex), you will have to use the *general mode*. Because integer mode is faster and requires less storage space on your computer, we suggest that you provide numeric codes for all variables or recode alphabetic codes to numeric codes. (See Chapter 3 for a description of the RECODE command.) Hence, we will use the integer mode in our subsequent descriptions. (If you wish to know more about the general mode, consult the *SPSS^x User's Guide,* under the index heading of "General Mode" in FREQUENCIES command.)

GENERAL FORMAT OF THE FREQUENCIES COMMAND

```
FREQUENCIES  VARIABLES=VARA (minimum value, maximum value)
```

First the command name for the procedure is specified: FREQUENCIES. This is followed by the subcommand VARIABLES= and a list of the variables for which frequency distributions are to be calculated. The names of variables in the VARIABLES= subcommand must correspond to the names given to those variables in the DATA LIST command. Each variable name in the VARIABLES= subcommand is followed by the specification, in parentheses, of the range of values being considered for that variable. Note that the subcommand is separated from the procedure command by at least one space.

Suppose, for example, that you wished to look at the frequency distribution of college students by class at a particular school. You would set up the frequency request as follows:

```
FREQUENCIES  VARIABLES=CLASS(1,4)
```

Using this specification, the variable CLASS has a range of values coded as 1, 2, 3, and 4. This could be used if you had coded your data in the following format: freshmen = 1, sophomores = 2, juniors = 3, and seniors = 4. Your output would be a frequency count (number and percentage) of the students in each class.

VARIATIONS IN FORMAT

If you are requesting frequency information on several variables, for example, class, sex, rank in class, and religious affiliation, you could use the following form:

```
FREQUENCIES  VARIABLES=CLASS(1,4) SEX(1,2) RANK(1,4) REL(0,4)
```

There are several things to notice here:

1. Spaces are used to separate the variables.
2. With a variable like class rank that has many possible values, you would probably want to code it into a limited set of discrete categories. You could do this when you establish your initial coding scheme on your data sheet or by using the RECODE command. You might use four categories: for example,

lowest quartile = 1, second quartile = 2, third quartile = 3, and highest quartile = 4. Thus the range of values for the variable called RANK would be 1 to 4 as shown in the example.

3. Similarly, you need a coding scheme for the variable of religious affiliation. You might use a five-category code: no response = 0, Protestant = 1, Roman Catholic = 2, Jewish = 3, other = 4.

Sometimes a variable may have decimal values, for example, grade point average. In that case, the program will truncate the decimal value to the lowest integer. A grade point average of 3.36 would become a 3; similarly, 3.75 would also become a 3. If you prefer not to leave this conversion up to the computer, you can develop your own coding scheme. You could use a scheme such as the following:

$$
\begin{array}{ll}
0-.50 = 1 & 2.01-2.50 = 5 \\
.51-1.00 = 2 & 2.51-3.00 = 6 \\
1.01-1.50 = 3 & 3.01-3.50 = 7 \\
1.51-2.00 = 4 & 3.51-4.00 = 8
\end{array}
$$

Your SPSS[x] command would then appear as:

```
FREQUENCIES  VARIABLES=GPA(1,8)
```

For a series of variables with the same response categories, you may use the word TO and place the minimum and maximum values after the last variable in the series. For example

```
FREQUENCIES  VAR1 TO VAR7(1,5) VAR8(0,3)
             VAR9 TO VAR13(0,9)
```

In this case, variables 1 through 7 have the same five response categories. Variable 8 has four response categories. Variables 9 through 13 are coded similarly with 10 response categories (0 through 9). The preceding command would cause frequency distributions of all 13 variables to be tabulated and printed. (Notice that continuation of a command to the next line requires at least one space of indentation.)

ADDITIONAL SUBCOMMANDS

Several optional subcommands may be used with the FREQUENCIES procedure to control the way the data are presented in the output. We will consider several that are commonly used.

FORMAT= Subcommand

Using this subcommand, you can arrange for the frequency tables to be presented in ways that are easily reproduced for reports. For example, to have the frequency tables produced so that they fit on a single page of the printout, you would use the following command:

```
FREQUENCIES  VARIABLES=VAR1(1,4) VAR2(0,3)/
             FORMAT=ONEPAGE
```

Notice that a slash (/) is needed to separate the VARIABLES= subcommand from the FORMAT= subcommand. The FORMAT= subcommand could have begun on the same line as the VARIABLE= subcommand (assuming there was sufficient space); however, your file is more readable when you use a new line for each new subcommand.

Some other FORMAT= choices and their functions are

```
FORMAT=NEWPAGE
```

Results in the printing of each new table on a new page of the printout.

```
FORMAT=AFREQ
```

Causes the categories on the frequency tables to be listed in ascending order of frequencies. The usual (i.e., default) arrangement is ascending order of values of the variables.

```
FORMAT=DFREQ
```

Causes the categories on the frequency tables to be listed in descending order of frequencies.

```
FORMAT=DVALUE
```

Causes the categories on the frequency tables to be listed in descending order of the values of the variables.

```
FORMAT=INDEX
```

Causes two indexes of the tables to be printed—one according to page order and one in alphabetic order of variable names.

Suppose that you wished to use several of these options in constructing your printout. You might specify the following:

```
FREQUENCIES  VARIABLES=VAR1(1,4) VAR2 TO VAR5(0,3)/
             FORMAT=NEWPAGE AFREQ INDEX
```

This would result in the printing of each table on a separate page, with table categories arranged in ascending order of frequencies. An index to the location of the tables in the printout would also be produced. Notice that a slash (/) separates the subcommands, and spaces separate the different FORMAT= options.

BARCHART= Subcommand

This subcommand results in a graphic chart of bars representing the frequency distribution of the values of a variable, the length of the bars denoting the number of cases for each value of the variable. (No bars occur for values having no cases.) Values and value labels are printed with the bars. The appropriate set of commands to obtain a bar chart is

```
FREQUENCIES  VARIABLES=VAR1(1,4) VAR2(0,3)/
             BARCHART
```

Notice that a slash (/) separates the VARIABLES= subcommand from the BARCHART subcommand. The BARCHART subcommand may be placed on the same line as the VARIABLES= subcommand if there is room, or it may be placed on the next line for ease in reading. Remember to indent at least one space when a command is continued on a new line.

Further specification may be made with BARCHART concerning the range of values to be plotted and whether percentages or actual frequencies are to be used. (Frequencies are used unless otherwise specified.) Some of the additional options with the BARCHART subcommand are listed as follows (and further descriptions may be obtained from the *SPSS^x User's Guide*).

```
BARCHART=MIN(n)
```

> Where *n* is the lowest value of the variable to be included on the bar chart if you do not wish to include all values.

```
BARCHART=MAX(n)
```

> Where *n* is the highest value of the variable to be included on the bar chart if you do not wish to include all values.

```
BARCHART=PERCENT(n)
```

> Which indicates that the horizontal axis of the bar chart will be labeled as percentages rather than as frequencies and that the maximum percentage will be *n*. If you do not specify a maximum percentage, the program will set an appropriate maximum at 5, 10, 25, 50, or 100, depending on the percentage of cases in the largest category.

To combine different options provided by the BARCHART= subcommand, you may use the following format:

```
FREQUENCIES  VAR1(1,20)/
             BARCHART=MIN(5) MAX(15)
```

Notice that a space separates the different choices included in the subcommand.

HISTOGRAM= Subcommand

This subcommand enables you to represent graphically your frequency distributions with histograms. The vertical axis of the graph represents the values of the variables. On the horizontal axis, asterisks (*) represent the number of cases falling into each category. For example, to have histograms printed, you would use the following format:

```
FREQUENCIES  VARIABLES=VAR1(1,4) VAR2(0,3)/
             HISTOGRAM
```

Other specifications may also be made with HISTOGRAM, such as placing limits on values to be plotted, scaling by percentages rather than frequencies, changing interval width, and superimposing the normal curve over the graph for comparison. These options are summarized as follows:

```
HISTOGRAM=MIN(n)
```
> Where n is the lowest value that you wish to have plotted for that variable.

```
HISTOGRAM=MAX(n)
```
> Where n is the highest value that you wish to have plotted for that variable.

```
HISTOGRAM=PERCENT(n)
```
> Specifies that the horizontal axis be represented in percentages with n as the maximum percentage listed. If n is not specified, the program will set an appropriate maximum from 5, 10, 25, 50, or 100 percent, according to the percentage of cases in the largest category.

```
HISTOGRAM=INCREMENT(n)
```
> Allows you to increase the number of response categories for the graph when you have more than 21 categories for a given variable. By default, SPSS^x is equipped to handle variables with up to 21 categories. If you have more than 21 categories and you do not wish to have these collapsed into 21 categories, you may specify a value n with this command, which will allow you to choose the number of categories you desire. SPSS^x divides n into the range of values for the given variable to produce the desired number of categories. For example, an n of 2 for a set of values ranging from 1 to 50 would result in 25 categories for the vertical axis of the graph. An n of 1 for values from 1 to 50 would produce 50 categories for the histogram.

```
HISTOGRAM=NORMAL
```
> Results in the superimposition of the normal curve over the obtained histogram.

To combine several of these options, you could use the following format:

```
FREQUENCIES  VARIABLES=VAR1(1,15)/
             HISTOGRAM=MIN(5) NORMAL
```

A space separates the different options chosen within the HISTOGRAM= subcommand.

PERCENTILES= Subcommand

To get the value of the variable representing a certain percentile, for example, the twenty-fifth percentile, the subcommand PERCEN-TILES=25 is used. Several percentiles can be requested at once. For example

```
FREQUENCIES  VARIABLES=VAR1(1,30)/
             PERCENTILES=25 50 75 33.3
```

For other variations, see the *SPSS^x User's Guide.*

STATISTICS= Subcommand

A variety of statistics may be requested with this command. Simply use the STATISTICS= designation and write in as many of the following keywords as you wish:

MEDIAN
MODE
MEAN
MINIMUM
MAXIMUM
STDDEV (standard deviation)
DEFAULT (gives mean, minimum, maxim   and standard deviation)

For example, you might request the following:

```
FREQUENCIES  VARIABLES=VAR1(1,10)/
             STATISTICS=MODE DEFAULT
```

Here we have requested the default statistics of mean, minimum, maximum, and standard deviation, and we have also requested the mode. Notice that a space separates the keywords. For additional statistics, consult the *SPSS^x User's Guide.*

USING MORE THAN ONE SUBCOMMAND

More than one subcommand may be used with FREQUENCIES. Each subcommand is separated from the next with a slash (/). They may be listed consecutively on the same line as long as there is room, or they may be placed on separate lines for ease in reading as long as you indent at least one space for each continuation line. In the following example, you can see two ways of typing in the same set of subcommands:

```
FREQUENCIES  VARIABLES=VAR1(1,30)/FORMAT=ONEPAGE/HISTOGRAM=PERCENT
             NORMAL/PERCENTILES=25 50 75/STATISTICS=DEFAULT
```

or

```
FREQUENCIES  VARIABLES=VAR1(1,30)/
             FORMAT=ONEPAGE/
             HISTOGRAM=PERCENT NORMAL/
             PERCENTILES=25 50 75/
             STATISTICS=DEFAULT
```

PUTTING THE SPSS^x FILE TOGETHER

Now try to write an SPSS^x file that constructs a frequency distribution for each of several variables. Suppose that you have obtained basic demographic data on a sample of 100 voters in your county, and you wish to develop a profile of voter characteristics. The variables that you will be looking at and their numeric codes are

Sex: female = 1, male = 2
Race: non-Caucasian = 1, Caucasian = 2
Party: Democratic = 1, Republican = 2, Independent = 3

Assuming that your data sheet looks like the one in Figure 5.1, try to write an SPSS^x file that creates a frequency distribution for each of the three variables. Afterward, check your completed SPSS^x file with the one in Figure 5.2.

Notes and Variations

```
DATA LIST   /SEX 5 RACE 6 PARTY 7
```

> If no identification code for the individual cases had been typed in, the variable values could have been located in different columns (e.g., starting in column 1) and the following DATA LIST command could have been used:
>
> ```
> DATA LIST   /SEX 1 RACE 2 PARTY 3
> ```

**FIGURE 5.1 Data Sheet for Frequency
Distributions of Voter
Characteristics**

ID	SEX	RACE	PARTY
001	1	2	3
002	1	2	1
003	2	1	2
.	.	.	.
.	.	.	.
100	1	2	3

FIGURE 5.2 SPSS× File for Frequency Distributions of Voter Characteristics

```
JOB...
EXEC SPSSX...              (JCL commands for your local computer system)
TITLE  "FREQUENCY DISTRIBUTIONS FOR VOTERS"
DATA LIST  /SEX 5 RACE 6 PARTY 7
VALUE LABELS  SEX 1 "FEMALE" 2 "MALE"/
              RACE 1 "NONCAUCASIAN" 2 "CAUCASIAN"/
              PARTY 1 "DEMOCRAT" 2 "REPUBLICAN" 3 "INDEPENDENT"
FREQUENCIES  VARIABLES=SEX(1,2) RACE(1,2) PARTY(1,3)
BEGIN DATA
001 123
002 121
003 212
 .
 .
 .
100 123
END DATA
FINISH
END OF JOB...              (JCL command for your computer system)
```

```
VALUE LABELS  SEX 1 "FEMALE" 2 "MALE"/
```

> This command is optional and could have been omitted. Its
> use, however, does make your printout more readable and
> accessible for future reference. Thus we encourage you to use
> this command.
>
> Sometimes a VARIABLE LABELS command is also needed if
> the abbreviated name of the variable is not self-evident (e.g.,
> SCORE1). Names such as SEX, AGE, and PARTY are more
> obvious and do not require expanded labels for the printout.

```
FREQUENCIES  VARIABLES=SEX(1,2) RACE(1,2) PARTY(1,3)
```

> In this first example, we have used the most general form of
> the FREQUENCIES command without specifying further
> options for the form of the printout or the statistics to be
> calculated. Without these additional specifications, your
> printout will contain tables of frequency and percentage values
> (actual frequency, percentage, valid percentage, and cumulative
> percentage), with the values arranged in ascending order and
> the number of missing cases reported.

Note: Variables listed in the **VALUE LABELS** and **FREQUENCIES** commands must be
spelled exactly as they appear in the **DATA LIST** command.

The next two examples will give you a chance to observe other variations in the use of the FREQUENCIES procedure. These examples also

include descriptions of relevant aspects of the outputs from the FRE-
QUENCIES procedures.

EXAMPLE 1: HEALTH PRETEST

Suppose that you have collected information from 30 new members of a
health club on their general health and current level of physical activity.
You plan to compare these findings with posttraining assessments to evaluate improvement as a result of the program at the club. Although an
extensive questionnaire would normally be administered, we will consider
only a few items for the sake of simplicity. Suppose that you have assessed
the following: subject sex, age, education, height, weight, resting heart
rate, and average amount of time spent in vigorous activity per day.

First you must establish numeric codes for categorizing the responses.
We might use the following:

Sex: male = 1, female = 2

Age: 18 and under = 1, 19 to 25 = 2, 26 to 35 = 3, 36 to 45 = 4, 46 and over
= 5, preferred not to answer = 6

Education: high school or less = 1, some college = 2, bachelor's degree = 3,
graduate degree = 4, preferred not to answer = 5

Height (in inches): 60 and under = 1, 61 to 66 = 2, 67 to 72 = 3, 73 to 79 = 4,
80 and over = 5

Weight (in pounds): 100 or less = 1, 101 to 120 = 2, 121 to 140 = 3, 141 to
160 = 4, 161 to 180 = 5, 181 and over = 6

Resting heart rate (in beats per minute): 60 and under = 1, 61 to 80 = 2, 81 to
100 = 3, 101 to 120 = 4, 121 and over = 5

Average daily activity time (in minutes): 15 and under = 1, 16 to 30 = 2, 31 to
60 = 3, 61 and over = 4

Appropriately coded, your data sheet might look like the one shown
in Figure 5.3, and your SPSS^x file would appear as shown in Figure 5.4.

FIGURE 5.3   Data Sheet for Health Pretest

SUBJECT	SEX	AGE	EDUCATION	HEIGHT	WEIGHT	HEART RATE	ACTIVITY TIME
01	1	2	3	2	3	2	2
02	1	1	3	3	4	3	1
03	2	3	4	2	3	3	1
.	.	.	.	.	.	.	.
.	.	.	.	.	.	.	.
30	1	3	5	4	5	3	1

FIGURE 5.4 SPSSˣ File for Health Pretest

```
JOB...
EXEC SPSSX...              (JCL commands for your computer system)
TITLE    "FREQUENCY DISTRIBUTIONS FOR HEALTH CLASS B1"
FILE HANDLE   HEALTHB1/local system specifications
DATA LIST    /SEX 4 AGE 5 ED 6 HT 7 WT 8 HR 9 ACTIV 10
MISSING VALUES   AGE (6) ED (5)
VARIABLE LABELS   ED "HIGHEST LEVEL COMPLETED"
                  HT "HEIGHT IN INCHES"
                  WT "WEIGHT IN POUNDS"
                  HR "RESTING HEART RATE IN BEATS PER MINUTE"
                  ACTIV "AVERAGE DAILY ACTIVITY IN MIN"
VALUE LABELS   SEX 1 "MALE" 2 "FEMALE"/
               AGE 1 "18 AND UNDER" 2 "19-25" 3 "26-35" 4 "36-45"
                   5 "46 AND OVER"/
               ED   1 "HIGH SCHOOL OR LESS" 2 "SOME COLLEGE"
                    3 "BACHELOR'S" 4 "GRADUATE DEGREE"/
               HT   1 "60 AND UNDER" 2 "61-66" 3 "67-72" 4 "73-79"
                    5 "80 AND OVER"/
               WT   1 "100 AND UNDER" 2 "101-120" 3 "121-140"
                    4 "141-160" 5 "161-180" 6 "181 AND OVER"/
               HR   1 "60 AND UNDER" 2 "61-80" 3 "81-100" 4 "101-120"
                    5 "121 AND OVER"/
               ACTIV 1 "15 AND UNDER" 2 "16-30" 3 "31-60"
                     4 "61 AND OVER"
FREQUENCIES   VARIABLES=SEX(1,2) AGE(1,5) ED(1,4) HT(1,5) WT(1,6)
                 HR(1,5) ACTIV(1,4)/
              FORMAT=ONEPAGE NEWPAGE INDEX/
              HISTOGRAM/
              STATISTICS=DEFAULT
BEGIN DATA
01 1232322
02 1133431
03 2342331
.
.
.
30 1354531
END DATA
SAVE    OUTFILE=HEALTHB1
FINISH
END OF JOB...             (JCL command for your computer system)
```

We have requested

1. Frequency tables for all variables, with those tables being presented one to a page
2. An index that identifies the locations of the tables in the printout
3. Histograms for all of the variables
4. Mean, minimum score, maximum score, and standard deviation for each variable

FIGURE 5.5   Partial Output for FREQUENCIES Procedure for Health Pretest

```
ED        HIGHEST LEVEL COMPLETED

                                                 VALID     CUM
    VALUE LABEL                VALUE  FREQUENCY  PERCENT  PERCENT  PERCENT

HIGH SCHOOL OR LESS              1        3       10.0     11.1     11.1
SOME COLLEGE                     2        3       10.0     11.1     22.2
BACHELORS'S                      3       12       40.0     44.4     66.7
GRADUATE DEGREE                  4        9       30.0     33.3    100.0
OUT OF RANGE                              3       10.0    MISSING
                                      -------   -------  -------
                          TOTAL          30      100.0    100.0

     COUNT      VALUE     ONE SYMBOL EQUALS APPROXIMATELY   .40 OCCURRENCES

        3       1.00   ********
        3       2.00   ********
       12       3.00   *********************************
        9       4.00   ***********************
                       I.........I.........I.........I.........I.........I
                       0         4         8        12        16        20
                                  HISTOGRAM FREQUENCY
MEAN            3.000   STD DEV        .961     MINIMUM       1.000
MAXIMUM         4.000

VALID CASES       27   MISSING CASES      3
```

We have also used the FILE HANDLE and SAVE commands to store the file for future retrieval, as shown in the next example.

Output from Health Pretest

The printout for the variable of ED is shown in Figure 5.5. Notice that four indices of frequency are given in the figure.

1. The absolute frequency or exact number of cases in each category, including missing data (out of range)
2. The relative frequency or percentage of total cases in each category, including missing data (out of range)
3. The adjusted frequency or percentages of cases in each category, excluding missing data (valid percent)
4. The cumulative adjusted frequency, excluding missing data

The histogram and statistics appear below the frequency table.

EXAMPLE 2: HEALTH PRETEST—ADDITIONAL ANALYSES

Suppose that you wished to perform the following transformations on your data before requesting frequency distributions:

1. Examine only the data from persons over 25
2. Recode education level into two categories: those with and without a college degree

LIMITATIONS OF FREQUENCIES

An upper limit of 500 variables can be specified with a single FREQUEN-CIES command. The maximum value range for a given integer variable is 32,767, and the maximum number of observed values over *all* variables included in the FREQUENCIES command is also 32,767. The only other restriction is imposed by the storage capacity of your local computer. In the unlikely event that one of these limits is exceeded, reduce the number of variables listed on the initial FREQUENCIES command and either use additional FREQUENCIES commands at the end of the data or use the GET procedure.

FIGURE 5.6 **File of Additional Analyses on Health Pretest**

```
JOB...
EXEC SPSSX...              (JCL commands for your computer system)
TITLE  "MODIFIED FREQUENCY DISTRIBUTIONS FOR HEALTH CLASS B1"
FILE HANDLE  HEALTHB1/local system specifications
GET  FILE=HEALTHB1
SELECT IF  (AGE GT 2)
RECODE  ED (LOWEST THRU 2=1) (3 THRU 4=2)
VALUE LABELS  ED 1 "NO BA" 2 "BA OR HIGHER"
FREQUENCIES  VARIABLES=SEX(1,2) AGE(3,5) ED(1,2) HT(1,5) WT(1,6)
             HR(1,5) ACTIV(1,4)/
             FORMAT=ONEPAGE NEWPAGE INDEX/
             HISTOGRAM/
             STATISTICS=DEFAULT
FINISH
END OF JOB...            (JCL command for your computer system)
```

Because you have already saved the Health Pretest data in SPSS^x system file HEALTHB1, you can use the GET command to perform the additional analyses. A file that contains the SPSS^x commands that would perform these additional analyses is presented in Figure 5.6. Notice that a VALUE LABELS command was included to relabel the new levels of variable ED.

The printout for the recoded variable of ED is shown in Figure 5.7. Note that only 15 cases are included as a result of the SELECT IF command and that ED is coded into two categories as specified. Three cases were found to be "out of range," that is, coded as missing data.

FIGURE 5.7 **Partial Output for Additional Analyses on Health Pretest**

```
ED        HIGHEST LEVEL COMPLETED

                                            VALID      CUM
   VALUE LABEL              VALUE  FREQUENCY  PERCENT  PERCENT  PERCENT
NO BA                         1       6       40.0     50.0     50.0
BA OR HIGHER                  2       6       40.0     50.0    100.0
OUT OF RANGE                  3       3       20.0    MISSING
                                    ------   ------   ------
                           TOTAL     15      100.0    100.0

    COUNT      VALUE    ONE SYMBOL EQUALS APPROXIMATELY    .20 OCCURRENCES
       6       1.00    *********************************
       6       2.00    *********************************
                       I.........I.........I.........I.........I.........I
                       0         2         4         6         8        10
                                   HISTOGRAM FREQUENCY
MEAN        1.500     STD DEV       .522     MINIMUM      1.000
MAXIMUM     2.000

VALID CASES    12     MISSING CASES     3
```

CROSSTABS: Contingency Table Analysis

PURPOSE

The CROSSTABS procedure is used to examine statistical relationships among variables that have discrete (discontinuous) values or a limited number of values. A joint frequency distribution is obtained in the form of a table—the crosstabulation table. In addition, the degree of association between variables may be determined through the use of statistical tests such as *chi-square* (χ^2) and *phi* (ϕ).

For instance, one might have obtained some demographic measures for a sample of persons, such as age categories and income levels. It would be possible, then, to examine the joint distribution of age and income as shown:

		AGE LEVELS		
		(1) UNDER 20	(2) 20 TO 65	(3) OVER 65
	(1) UNDER 10,000			
INCOME	(2) 10,000 TO 50,000			
	(3) OVER 50,000			

This table would reveal the number and percentage of persons in the sample who are under 20 and have incomes under $10,000; the number of persons who have incomes under $10,000 and are between 20 and 65 years of age; and so on. In addition, one could find out whether the pattern of joint frequencies for these variables reveals a relationship between them that is significantly different from chance. For example, does income increase directly with age? To determine this, you could request a statistical test such as chi-square.

CHOOSING INTEGER VERSUS GENERAL MODES FOR THE CROSSTABS PROCEDURE

There are two possible ways to set up the CROSSTABS procedure. One, called the integer mode, is used if all response categories for the variables are coded numerically (e.g., codes of 1 and 2 for male and female subjects, respectively). The other, called the general mode, is used if you have some response categories with alphabetic codes (e.g., codes of M and F for male and female subjects, respectively). Because the integer mode is faster and requires less storage capacity on your computer, we suggest that you use it and provide numeric codes for all response categories. If you have already created alphabetic codes for your data, use the RECODE command to convert these to numeric codes. In the sections that follow, we will describe the use of the integer mode. (If you wish to know more about using the general mode for the CROSSTABS procedure, consult *SPSS^x User's Guide.*)

GENERAL FORMAT OF THE CROSSTABS COMMAND

$$\text{CROSSTABS} \quad \text{VARIABLES=VARA} \left(\begin{array}{c} \text{minimum maximum} \\ \text{value , value} \end{array} \right) \text{VARB} \left(\begin{array}{c} \text{minimum maximum} \\ \text{value , value} \end{array} \right) /$$
$$\text{TABLES=VARA BY VARB}$$

The specification part of the command contains two kinds of information:

1. The VARIABLES= subcommand specifies all of the variables for which crosstabulations are to be performed. The name of each variable (which must be identical to the name used in the DATA LIST command) is followed by the minimum and maximum values (i.e., the lowest and highest levels) being considered for that variable. The list of variables is followed by a slash (/).
2. The TABLES= subcommand specifies all of the crosstabulation tables desired. The variables included in this statement must also appear in the VARIABLES= subcommand.

To use our previous example involving age and income, we would request the 3 by 3 crosstabulation table shown with the following command:

```
CROSSTABS  VARIABLES=AGE (1,3) INCOME (1,3)/
           TABLES=AGE BY INCOME
```

VARIATIONS IN FORMAT

VARIABLES= Subcommand

If several variables have the same number of response categories and the same minimum and maximum values are being considered, you may put the minimum and maximum values once at the end of the group of variables having the same values. Alternatively, you could use the word TO to specify a sequence of variables from the DATA LIST. For example, instead of the following CROSSTABS command that fully specifies such a sequence

```
CROSSTABS  VARIABLES=SEX (1,2) AGE (1,3) INCOME (1,3) OCCUP (1,3)
           MARITAL (1,3) VOTE (1,5)/
```

you could use either of the following formats:

```
CROSSTABS  VARIABLES=SEX (1,2) AGE INCOME OCCUP MARITAL (1,3) VOTE
           (1,5)/
CROSSTABS  VARIABLES=SEX (1,2) AGE TO MARITAL (1,3) VOTE (1,5)/
```

TABLES= Subcommand

You may request one or more crosstabulation tables with the TABLES= subcommand. Variables involved in the tables may have differing numbers of response categories. One way to request several two-way tables with one variable in common is the following:

```
CROSSTABS  VARIABLES=SEX (1,3) AGE INCOME OCCUP (1,3) VOTE (1,5)/
           TABLES=SEX BY AGE INCOME OCCUP VOTE
```

This procedure would yield the following four tables: SEX by AGE, SEX by INCOME, SEX by OCCUP, SEX by VOTE. You could also use the word TO to shorten the listing of crosstabulation tables as shown:

```
CROSSTABS  VARIABLES=SEX (1,2) AGE INCOME OCCUP (1,3) VOTE (1,5)/
           TABLES=SEX BY AGE TO VOTE
```

You may use a combination of the preceding variations. For example

```
CROSSTABS  VARIABLES=VARA (1,2) VARB TO VARF (1,4) VARG (0,3) VARH
           (1,3)/
           TABLES=VARA BY VARB VARC VARF TO VARH
```

which would yield five tables: VARA by VARB, VARA by VARC, VARA by VARF, VARA by VARG, and VARA by VARH.

In addition, you are not limited to two-way tables but may request three-way, four-way, or larger tables (up to a maximum of eight-way). For example, you might wish to examine a three-way joint frequency distribution of AGE by SEX by INCOME.

To request more than two variables in the crosstabulation table, you simply extend the list with the word BY:

```
CROSSTABS  VARIABLES=SEX (1,2) AGE INCOME (1,3) VOTE (1,5)/
           TABLES=SEX BY AGE BY INCOME
```

To request more than one crosstabulation table, use slashes (/) to separate the requests:

```
CROSSTABS  VARIABLES=SEX (1,2) AGE 1NCOME (1,3) VOTE (1,5)/
           TABLES=SEX BY AGE BY INCOME/
           SEX BY VOTE/
           AGE BY VOTE
```

As you will notice when you view your output, crosstabulation tables are constructed as two dimensional. Thus the preceding command would result in three SEX by AGE tables—one for each level of INCOME.

Similarly, a request for

```
CROSSTABS  VARIABLES=VARA TO VARD (1,2)/
           TABLES=VARA BY VARB BY VARC BY VARD
```

would produce four two-way tables as follows:

1. VARA by VARB for level 1 of VARC and level 1 of VARD
2. VARA by VARB for level 2 of VARC and level 1 of VARD
3. VARA by VARB for level 1 of VARC and level 2 of VARD
4. VARA by VARB for level 2 of VARC and level 2 of VARD

COMMONLY USED OPTIONS

There are 18 OPTIONS available with CROSSTABS. (See the CROSS-TABS chapter in *SPSS^x User's Guide*.) The OPTIONS command, if used, follows the CROSSTABS command. You may specify some or none of these in your SPSS^x file. Some of the more commonly used options follow:

```
OPTIONS  1
```

> Causes all codes to be included in the tables and statistics—even those for missing data (e.g., a category designated as "no response" and treated as a missing value).
>
> If this option is not used, data coded as missing will be excluded from the tables and the number of instances of missing data will be reported separately in the printout.

```
OPTIONS 3
```
>   Causes cell frequencies to be reported as percentages of the
>   row total.

```
OPTIONS 4
```
>   Causes cell frequencies to be reported as percentages of the
>   column total.

```
OPTIONS 5
```
>   Causes cell frequencies to be reported as percentages of the
>   total number of cases in the table.

```
OPTIONS 7
```
>   Causes missing values to be included in the tables but not in
>   the statistical tests.

```
OPTIONS 9
```
>   Causes a reference index to be printed, specifying the location
>   of each table in the printout by page number. This option is
>   quite useful when requesting a large number of tables.

```
OPTIONS 14
```
>   Causes the expected frequencies (i.e., the frequencies expected
>   on the basis of chance) for each cell to be printed.

```
OPTIONS 18
```
>   Causes all available information to be printed: cell frequencies;
>   row, column, and table percentages; expected values and
>   associated residuals.

To invoke more than one option, simply list the desired option numbers, separated by spaces, in the specification portion of the OPTIONS command:

```
OPTIONS 1 7 9
```

You may omit the OPTIONS command altogether if you do not wish to use any of the possible options.

COMMONLY USED STATISTICS

There are 11 statistical tests that may be used with CROSSTABS. You need to list the numbers of the desired statistics in the specification portion of the STATISTICS command. The STATISTICS command, if used, follows the OPTIONS command. The possible statistical tests are:

1. Yates' corrected chi-square (or Fisher's exact test for 2 × 2 tables with fewer than 21 cases)
2. Phi for 2 × 2 tables or Cramer's *V* for larger tables
3. Contingency coefficient
4. Lambda, symmetric and asymmetric
5. Uncertainty coefficient, symmetric and asymmetric
6. Kendall's tau *b*
7. Kendall's tau *c*
8. Gamma (partial and zero order gamma for three- to *n*-variable tables)
9. Somer's D, symmetric and asymmetric
10. Eta
11. Pearson product-moment correlation coefficient (*r*) for numeric data

Thus, a command like

```
STATISTICS 1 3 6
```

would result in the computation of three statistical tests—chi-square, contingency coefficient, and Kendall's tau *b*—for each crosstabulation table listed. If all of the statistical tests are appropriate and desired, put the word ALL in the specification field as shown:

```
STATISTICS ALL
```

If no statistics are desired, omit the STATISTICS command altogether.

PUTTING THE SPSSˣ FILE TOGETHER

Now try to construct an SPSSˣ file for a simple crosstabulation procedure. Suppose that you have collected data from 1000 randomly selected respondents who are married and over the age of 35. You are examining the relationship between their religious affiliation and the number of children they have. The data have been coded as follows:

> Religious affiliation: Catholic = 1, Jewish = 2, Protestant = 3, other = 4, none = 5
>
> Number of children: no children = 0, one child = 1, two children = 2, three children = 3, four or more children = 4

Your data sheet might look like that shown in Figure 6.1. Try to write an SPSSˣ file that performs a crosstabulation between these two variables and then check it with the one in Figure 6.2.

Notes and Variations

DATA LIST   /RELIGION 6 CHILDREN 7

>Because a four-digit identification code and a blank space were included before the data codes for each respondent, the data do not appear until columns 6 and 7. There are alternative ways of typing in the data—for instance, not including an identification code. Whatever format you choose, it must be

FIGURE 6.1   Data Sheet for Crosstabulation of Religion with Family Size

RESPONDENT	RELIGIOUS AFFILIATION	NUMBER OF CHILDREN
0001	3	0
0002	1	2
0003	1	2
.	.	.
.	.	.
.	.	.
1000	2	4

FIGURE 6.2   SPSS^x File for Crosstabulations on Religion and Family Size

```
JOB. . .
EXEC SPSSX. . .                (JCL commands for your computer system)
TITLE  "CROSSTABS ON RELIGION AND FAMILY SIZE"
DATA LIST  /RELIGION 6 CHILDREN 7
VALUE LABELS    RELIGION 1 "CATHOLIC" 2 "JEWISH" 3 "PROTESTANT" 4 "OTHER"
                5 "NONE"/
                CHILDREN 1 "ONE CHILD" 2 "TWO CHILDREN" 3 "THREE CHILDREN"
                4 "FOUR OR MORE CHILDREN"
CROSSTABS  VARIABLES=RELIGION (1,5) CHILDREN (1,4)/
           TABLES=RELIGION BY CHILDREN
OPTIONS  3 4 9
STATISTICS  1
BEGIN DATA
0001 30
0002 12
0003 12
  .
  .
  .
1000 24
END DATA
FINISH
END OF JOB. . .               (JCL command for your computer)
```

clearly indicated in the DATA LIST command. For example, if the data had been typed in the following form:

(Columns 12)

    30
    12
    12

    .
    .
    .

    24

the DATA LIST command would look like this:

```
DATA LIST  /RELIGION 1 CHILDREN 2
```

```
VALUE LABELS  RELIGION 1 "CATHOLIC" 2 "JEWISH" 3 "PROTESTANT"
4 "OTHER" 5 "NONE"/
```

The VALUE LABELS command is optional. In this case, it seemed useful to identify the codes for the responses to the two variables; otherwise, your printout would contain only the numeric codes and would be more difficult to read and understand at a glance. Also optional is the VARIABLE LABELS command, which we chose to omit because the variable names are sufficiently descriptive.

```
OPTIONS  3 4 9
```

The OPTIONS command requests the printing of row and column percentages and the construction of an index to table locations in the printout.

```
STATISTICS  1
```

The statistics command requests the computation of the chi-square statistic for the crosstabulation table. Other statistics are also available as described earlier.

Note that the variables listed in the VALUE LABELS and CROSSTABS commands *must be spelled exactly* as they appear in the DATA LIST statement.

After you understand the logic of this example, you should continue with the following more complex examples that demonstrate other choices and variations available with the procedure.

EXAMPLE 1: VOTER CHARACTERISTICS

Suppose that, to understand voting behavior better, you have obtained a variety of measures on a random sample of voters in the last gubernatorial

FIGURE 6.3   Data Sheet for Voter Characteristics

SUJBECT	SEX	AGE	EDUCATION	INCOME	RACE	PARTY	OCCUPATION	VOTE
001	1	2	3	2	3	2	2	1
002	1	2	4	3	1	1	2	2
003	2	3	1	4	1	1	3	2
.	.	.	.	.	.	.	.	.
.	.	.	.	.	.	.	.	.
.	.	.	.	.	.	.	.	.
100	2	4	2	3	3	2	3	1

election. You wish to look for variables that might be significantly related to the voting choices in that election. For the sake of simplicity, assume that we have obtained eight measures on each of 100 subjects in the sample. The eight variables and their numerically coded response categories are:

Sex: male = 1, female = 2
Age: 25 and under = 1, 26 to 40 = 2, 41 to 65 = 3, over 65 = 4
Education: high school or less = 1, some college = 2, college degree = 3, graduate degree = 4
Income: under 10,000 = 1, 10,000 to 29,999 = 2, 30,000 to 49,999 = 3, 50,000 and above = 4
Race: Black = 1, Hispanic = 2, Caucasian = 3, other = 4
Party affiliation: Democratic = 1, Republican = 2, other = 3, no party affiliation = 4
Occupation: labor = 1, white collar = 2, professional = 3
Vote: Jones = 1, Smith = 2, write-in = 3, did not vote = 4

A data sheet for this study might look like that shown in Figure 6.3.

To determine whether any of the variables (or some combinations of them) are significantly related to voting behavior, we could set up an SPSS^x file as shown in Figure 6.4.

We have requested three two-way crosstabulations—voting choice with sex, age, and education level. In addition, we have requested one three-way table: voting choice by age by educational level. The selected options cause all cell information to be printed (e.g., frequencies, percentages, expected values) and provide for a reference index. Chi-square (or Fisher's exact test) and phi (or Cramer's *V*) have been selected as the statistical tests. Notice that the MISSING VALUES command causes zeros coded on the data lines to be considered as missing data, that is, no response coded. We have also specified a FILE HANDLE for this file and saved the file for further analyses at a later time.

Output from CROSSTABS Procedure

A partial printout for this SPSS^x file showing a two-way crosstabulation between VOTE and SEX is presented in Figure 6.5. For the

FIGURE 6.4   SPSSˣ File for Voter Characteristics

```
JOB. . .
EXEC SPSSX. . .              (JCL commands for your computer system)
TITLE   "CROSSTABULATIONS ON VOTING"
FILE HANDLE   VOTER/local system specifications
DATA LIST   /SEX 5 AGE 6 EDUC 7 INCOME 8 RACE 9 PARTY 10 OCCUP 11 VOTE 12
MISSING VALUES   ALL (0)
VARIABLE LABELS   INCOME "ANNUAL FAMILY INCOME"
                  OCCUP "OCCUPATIONAL STATUS"
                  VOTE "CHOICE FOR GOVERNOR"
VALUE LABELS   SEX 1 "MALE" 2 "FEMALE"/
               AGE 1 "25 AND UNDER" 2 "26-40" 3 "41-65" 4 "OVER 65"/
               EDUC 1 "HIGH SCHOOL OR LESS" 2 "SOME COLLEGE" 3 "COLLEGE
               DEGREE" 4 "GRADUATE DEGREE"/
               INCOME 1 "UNDER 10,000" 2 "10,000-29,999" 3 "30,000-
               49,999" 4 "50,000 AND ABOVE" /
               RACE 1 "BLACK" 2 "HISPANIC" 3 "CAUCASIAN" 4 "OTHER"/
               PARTY 1 "DEMO" 2 "REPUB" 3 "OTHER" 4 "NONE"/
               OCCUP 1 "LABOR" 2 "WHITE COLLAR" 3 "PROFESSIONAL"/
               VOTE 1 "JONES" 2 "SMITH" 3 "WRITE IN" 4 "DID NOT VOTE"
CROSSTABS   VARIABLES=SEX (1,2) AGE TO PARTY (1,4) OCCUP (1,3) VOTE
            (1,4)/
            TABLES=VOTE BY SEX AGE EDUC/
            VOTE BY AGE BY EDUC
OPTIONS  9 18
STATISTICS  1 2
BEGIN DATA
001 12323221
002 12431122
003 23141132
 .
 .
 .
100 24233231
END DATA
SAVE  OUTFILE=VOTER
FINISH
END OF JOB. . .             (JCL command for your computer system)
```

crosstabulation of SEX by VOTE, a significant chi-square of 47.91667 ($p < .001$) was obtained, with Cramer's V indicating a relationship coefficient of .69222. Notice that each cell of the table contains eight numbers (as a result of OPTIONS 18). Reading from top to bottom, these numbers represent the actual number of persons in that category, the expected frequency for that category, the percentage of the row total falling in that category, the percentage of the column total falling in that category, the percentage of the total sample falling in that category, the residual (actual minus expected frequency), the standardized residuals, and the adjusted

FIGURE 6.5 Partial Output of CROSSTABS Procedure: VOTE BY SEX Table

```
- - - - - - - - - - - - - - - - - - - -  C R O S S T A B U L A T I O N   O F  - - - - - -
    VOTE        CHOICE FOR GOVERNOR                           BY  SEX
- - - - - - - - - - - - - - - - - - - - - - - - - - - - - - - - - - - - - - - - - - - - -
                        SEX
              COUNT   I
              EXP VAL I
              ROW PCT I
              COL PCT I
              TOT PCT I
              RESIDUAL IMALE       FEMALE     ROW
              STD RES I                       TOTAL
              ADJ RES I       1I        2I
VOTE          --------+--------+--------+
            1 I    30   I   10   I     40
JONES         I  24.0  I  16.0  I   40.0% *
              I  75.0% I  25.0% I
              I  50.0% I  25.0% I
              I  30.0% I  10.0% I
              I   6.0  I  -6.0  I
              I   1.2  I  -1.5  I
              I   2.5  I  -2.5  I
              +--------+--------+
            2 I    10   I   10   I     20
SMITH         I  12.0  I   8.0  I   20.0%
              I  50.0% I  50.0% I
              I  16.7% I  25.0% I
              I  10.0% I  10.0% I
              I  -2.0  I   2.0  I
              I   -.6  I    .7  I
              I  -1.0  I   1.0  I
              +--------+--------+
            3 I     0   I   20   I     20
WRITE IN      I  12.0  I   8.0  I   20.0%
              I   .0%  I 100.0% I
              I   .0%  I  50.0% I
              I   .0%  I  20.0% I
              I -12.0  I  12.0  I
              I  -3.5  I   4.2  I
              I  -6.1  I   6.1  I
              +--------+--------+
            4 I    20   I    0   I     20
DID NOT VOTE  I  12.0  I   8.0  I   20.0%
              I 100.0% I   .0%  I
              I  33.3% I   .0%  I
              I  20.0% I   .0%  I
              I   8.0  I  -8.0  I
              I   2.3  I  -2.8  I
              I   4.1  I  -4.1  I
              +--------+--------+
     COLUMN       60       40      100
     TOTAL      60.0%    40.0%   100.0%


CHI-SQUARE    D.F.      SIGNIFICANCE       MIN E.F.    CELLS WITH E.F.< 5
----------    ----      ------------       --------    ------------------

 47.91667      3          0.0000            8.000            NONE

      STATISTIC                   VALUE         SIGNIFICANCE
      ---------                   -----         ------------

CRAMER'S V                       0.69222

NUMBER OF MISSING OBSERVATIONS =      0
```

standardized residuals. Row and column marginal totals and percentages are also given.

In Figure 6.6, a partial output from one of the three-way crosstabulations is shown. We requested VOTE BY AGE BY EDUC. This is presented as a series of VOTE BY AGE tables for each value of EDUC. Figure 6.6 contains results for levels 1 and 2 of EDUC. Notice that when the separate tables were presented for different levels of education, some of the response categories for the other two variables had no cases and thus were excluded from the tables. You can also see that for these 2 by 2 tables with fewer cases, the appropriate statistics are Fisher's exact test and phi.

If cell frequencies are distributed in unusual ways that may affect

FIGURE 6.6   Partial Output of CROSSTABS Procedure: VOTE BY AGE BY EDUC Table

```
- - - - - - - - - - - - - - - - -   C R O S S T A B U L A T I O N   O F   - - - - - - - - -
   VOTE      CHOICE FOR GOVERNOR                            BY   AGE
CONTROLLING FOR..
   EDUC                                                     VALUE..   1   HIGH SCHOOL OR LESS
- - - - - - - - - - - - - - - - - - - - - - - - - - - - - - - - - - - - - - - - - - - - - -

                       AGE
              COUNT  I
              EXP VAL I
              ROW PCT I
              COL PCT I
              TOT PCT I
              RESIDUALI25 AND U 41-65      ROW
              STD RES INDER                TOTAL
              ADJ RES I      1I       3I
   VOTE       --------+--------+--------+
           1  I     10   I     0   I    10
   JONES       I    5.0  I    5.0  I   50.0%
               I  100.0% I    .0%  I
               I  100.0% I    .0%  I
               I   50.0% I    .0%  I
               I    5.0  I   -5.0  I
               I    2.2  I   -2.2  I
               I    4.5  I   -4.5  I
               +--------+--------+
           2  I      0   I    10   I    10
   SMITH       I    5.0  I    5.0  I   50.0%
               I    .0%  I  100.0% I
               I    .0%  I  100.0% I
               I    .0%  I   50.0% I
               I   -5.0  I    5.0  I
               I   -2.2  I    2.2  I
               I   -4.5  I    4.5  I
               +--------+--------+
          COLUMN      10        10        20
          TOTAL    50.0%     50.0%    100.0%


          STATISTIC                 ONE TAIL        TWO TAIL
          ---------                 --------        --------

   FISHER'S EXACT TEST               0.00001         0.00001

          STATISTIC                 VALUE         SIGNIFICANCE
          ---------                 -----         ------------

   PHI                             1.00000


- - - - - - - - - - - - - - - - -   C R O S S T A B U L A T I O N   O F   - - - - - - - -
   VOTE      CHOICE FOR GOVERNOR                            BY   AGE
CONTROLLING FOR..
   EDUC                                                     VALUE..   2   SOME COLLEGE
- - - - - - - - - - - - - - - - - - - - - - - - - - - - - - - - - - - - - - - - - - - -

                       AGE
              COUNT  I
              EXP VAL I
              ROW PCT I
              COL PCT I
              TOT PCT I
              RESIDUALI41-65    OVER 65    ROW
              STD RES I                    TOTAL
              ADJ RES I      3I       4I
   VOTE       --------+--------+--------+
           1  I      0   I    10   I    10
   JONES       I    5.0  I    5.0  I   50.0%
               I    .0%  I  100.0% I
               I    .0%  I  100.0% I
               I    .0%  I   50.0% I
               I   -5.0  I    5.0  I
               I   -2.2  I    2.2  I
               I   -4.5  I    4.5  I
               +--------+--------+
           4  I     10   I     0   I    10
   DID NOT VOTE I    5.0  I    5.0  I   50.0%
               I  100.0% I    .0%  I
               I  100.0% I    .0%  I
               I   50.0% I    .0%  I
               I    5.0  I   -5.0  I
               I    2.2  I   -2.2  I
               I    4.5  I   -4.5  I
               +--------+--------+
          COLUMN      10        10        20
          TOTAL    50.0%     50.0%    100.0%


          STATISTIC                 ONE TAIL        TWO TAIL
          ---------                 --------        --------

   FISHER'S EXACT TEST               0.00001         0.00001

          STATISTIC                 VALUE         SIGNIFICANCE
          ---------                 -----         ------------

   PHI                             1.00000
```

FIGURE 6.7   SPSSˣ File of Additional Analyses on Voter Characteristics

```
JOB. . .
EXEC SPSSX. . .              (JCL commands for your computer system)
TITLE   "MODIFIED CROSSTABS ON VOTERS"
FILE HANDLE  VOTER/local system specifications
GET  FILE=VOTER
SELECT IF  (SEX EQ 1 AND AGE GE 2)
RECODE  RACE(1,2,4=1) (3=2)
VALUE LABELS  RACE 1 "NONCAUCASIAN" 2 "CAUCASIAN"
CROSSTABS  VARIABLES=AGE (2,4) EDUC (1,4) INCOME (1,4) RACE (1,2) PARTY
           (1,4) OCCUP (1,3) VOTE (1,4)/
           TABLES=VOTE BY RACE BY AGE
OPTIONS  9 18
STATISTICS  1 2
FINISH
END OF JOB. . .             (JCL command for your computer system)
```

interpretation, the output will contain appropriate messages, for example, the number of cells with expected frequencies less than 5.

EXAMPLE 2: VOTER CHARACTERISTICS—ADDITIONAL ANALYSES

Suppose that you wished to limit your analyses to male voters over the age of 25. Further, suppose you wished to recode RACE into Caucasian and non-Caucasian. The simplest way to do this is to access your system file that has been saved under the name VOTER, perform the data transformations, and then request new crosstabulation tables. The SPSSˣ file to invoke these changes is shown in Figure 6.7, and a partial output appears in Figure 6.8. Note the addition of a new VALUE LABELS command for the change related to race, and notice also that the SELECT IF command is used to select only the male voters over 25. Finally, these changes must also be made in the VARIABLES= list to accommodate the changes caused by the SELECT IF and RECODE commands (i.e., SEX is no longer a variable, and the minimum and maximum values of AGE and RACE have changed).

LIMITATIONS OF CROSSTABS

There are several specific limits related to the use of the integer mode of the CROSSTABS procedure.

FIGURE 6.8   Partial Crosstabulation Table for VOTE BY RACE (Recoded) BY AGE for Male Voters

```
- - - - - - - - - - - - - - - - - - -  C R O S S T A B U L A T I O N   O F  - - - -
  VOTE      CHOICE FOR GOVERNOR                              BY  RACE
CONTROLLING FOR..
  AGE                                                    VALUE..    2   26-40
- - - - - - - - - - - - - - - - - - - - - - - - - - - - - - - - - - - - - - - - - -

                     RACE
           COUNT   I
           EXP VAL I
           ROW PCT I
           COL PCT I
           TOT PCT I
           RESIDUAL INONCAUCA CAUCASIA   ROW
           STD RES  ISIAN       N       TOTAL
           ADJ RES I      1I        2I
 VOTE      --------+--------+--------+
             1  I      0  I     10  I     10
 JONES         I    5.0  I    5.0  I   50.0%
               I    .0%  I 100.0%  I
               I    .0%  I 100.0%  I
               I    .0%  I  50.0%  I
               I   -5.0  I    5.0  I
               I   -2.2  I    2.2  I
               I   -4.5  I    4.5  I
            +--------+--------+
             2  I     10  I      0  I     10
 SMITH         I    5.0  I    5.0  I   50.0%
               I 100.0%  I    .0%  I
               I 100.0%  I    .0%  I
               I  50.0%  I    .0%  I
               I    5.0  I   -5.0  I
               I    2.2  I   -2.2  I
               I    4.5  I   -4.5  I
            +--------+--------+
            COLUMN      10       10       20
            TOTAL     50.0%    50.0%   100.0%


        STATISTIC              ONE TAIL           TWO TAIL
        ---------              --------           --------

FISHER'S EXACT TEST            0.00001            0.00001

        STATISTIC               VALUE          SIGNIFICANCE
        ---------               -----          ------------

 PHI                          1.00000
```

1. No more than 100 variables can be included in either the VARIABLES= or the TABLES= portions of the CROSSTABS command. In the TABLES= portion, each repetition of a variable name is counted as an additional variable.

2. No variable can have more than 200 different values or response categories printed in tables or subtables.

3. Only 20 table requests (between slashes) may be invoked, although a given request may contain several tables.

4. The maximum number of dimensions available for any CROSSTABS procedure is eight (i.e., an eight-way table).

5. The largest *range* of values acceptable for a given variable is 32,766 (i.e., from minimum to maximum value defined on VARIABLES= subcommand).

There is also the possibility that you may exceed the storage capacity of your computer before reaching the preceding limits. In this case, reduce the number of variables or table requests on the CROSSTABS command and use additional CROSSTABS commands at the end of the data. As an alternative, you may use the GET procedure (shown in Figure 6.7). (See the CROSSTABS chapter in the *SPSS^x User's Guide* for further explanations of limitations.)

7

T-TEST: Student's *t*-test for Between-Subjects Designs

PURPOSE

T-TEST is the SPSS^x procedure that computes Student's *t*-test. This test is used to examine the effects of one independent variable on one or more dependent variables and is restricted to comparisons of *two* conditions or groups (two levels of the independent variable). The results of this test enable you to determine if two means differ significantly. Two basic experimental designs, between-subjects and within-subjects designs, can be analyzed with the T-TEST procedure. In this chapter, we will describe how to use the T-TEST procedure to analyze the results of between-subjects designs. It is important to distinguish between these two types of designs because they require different statistical procedures and thus different forms of the T-TEST command. In the next chapter, we describe how the T-TEST procedure can be used to analyze within-subjects designs.

A two-group between-subjects design is one in which participants have been randomly assigned to the two levels of the independent variable. In this design, each participant is assigned to only one group, and consequently, the two groups are independent of one another. For example, assume that you are interested in studying the effects of two types of drugs (X,Y) on reaction time. If you randomly assign some subjects to the Drug X group and other subjects to the Drug Y group, then you are using a between-subjects design. (If you desire further clarification of the distinction between a within- and a between-subjects design, compare the preceding description of a between-subjects design with the description of a within-subjects design in the next chapter.)

GENERAL FORMAT AND VARIATIONS FOR THE T-TEST COMMAND

The general format for the T-TEST procedure is

```
T-TEST  GROUPS=independent variable/VARIABLES=dependent variable(s)
```

As shown, the GROUPS= and the VARIABLES= subcommands follow the T-TEST command and are separated by a slash (/). With this format, it is assumed that values of 1 or 2 have been typed on the data lines to identify the treatment condition of each case or subject. Any case not assigned a value of 1 or 2 will be excluded from the analysis. For example, assume that you are testing the effects of massed versus distributed practice (TYPE-PRAC) on a motor response (MOTOR1). If subjects who participate under massed practice are assigned the value of 1 for the independent variable TYPEPRAC and subjects who receive distributed practice are assigned the value of 2, then the following format is appropriate:

```
T-TEST  GROUPS=TYPEPRAC/VARIABLES=MOTOR1
```

To perform T-TEST analyses on several dependent measures (e.g., MOTOR1, MOTOR2, MOTOR3, and MOTOR4), appropriate formats are

```
T-TEST  GROUPS=TYPEPRAC/VARIABLES=MOTOR1 MOTOR2 MOTOR3 MOTOR4
```

or

```
T-TEST  GROUPS=TYPEPRAC/VARIABLES=MOTOR1 TO MOTOR4
```

The results for these analyses would yield four separate *t*-tests, one for each of the four dependent measures. A maximum of 50 dependent variables can be listed after the VARIABLES= subcommand.

In the event that the values of the two levels of your independent variable are coded as something other than 1 or 2, then you must specify these values in the T-TEST command. The following general format would be used:

```
T-TEST  GROUPS= independent    (value x,value y)/VARIABLES= dependent
                 variable                                    variable(s)
```

For example, if you used the value 3 to code subjects in the massed practice condition and the value 6 to code subjects in the distributed practice condition, then the following format would be used:

```
T-TEST  GROUPS=TYPEPRAC(3,6)/VARIABLES=MOTOR1
```

In this instance, cases that have a value of 3 for variable TYPEPRAC will be assigned to Group 1 and cases that a have a value of 6 for variable TYPE-PRAC will be assigned to Group 2.

Finally, if the independent variable has more than two levels and you wish to combine some of the levels to form two groups for the *t*-test, the following format can be used:

```
T-TEST  GROUPS=independent variable (value)/VARIABLES=  dependent
                                                        variable(s)
```

The value in parentheses represents the dividing point between the two groups of independent variable levels; that is, one group is formed by the independent variable levels with codes *below* that value and the other group is formed by the independent variable levels coded *at* or *above* that value. This format enables you to compare the mean of all subjects whose treatment conditions are coded higher than or equal to a particular value with all subjects whose treatment conditions are coded lower than that value.

For example, if you had six levels of the TYPEPRAC variable in your experiment and you wished to compare the combined mean of conditions 4, 5, and 6 with the combined mean of conditions 1, 2, and 3, then the following format would be appropriate:

```
T-TEST  GROUPS=TYPEPRAC(4)/VARIABLES=MOTOR1
```

COMMONLY USED OPTIONS

Three OPTIONS are often used with the T-TEST procedure, and you may include some or none of these in your SPSS[x] file. If you desire to invoke an option, then the OPTIONS command should follow the T-TEST command and the following format should be used:

```
OPTIONS  1
```

Causes all previous MISSING VALUES commands to be ignored. Therefore, *all* of the data would be included in the analysis—even those with codes representing missing data.

```
OPTIONS  2
```

Causes a case to be eliminated from the analysis entirely if that case contains missing data on any of the variables that are listed in a given VARIABLES= subcommand.

If neither of these options is included, then the *default option* for missing data is in effect. The default option causes a missing score to be excluded only from the analysis involving that missing score. For example, if three *t*-tests were to be performed (each on a different dependent measure—A, B, and C) and if a particular subject had a missing score for only variable B, then that subject would be excluded only from the analysis involving variable B.

OPTIONS 4

Causes the computer to print the results within 80 columns.

If no options are desired, omit the OPTIONS command altogether.

STATISTICS

No optional statistics are available with the T-TEST procedure. (Thus you should not include a STATISTICS command.) In a normal run of the T-TEST procedure, several statistics will automatically be computed, and these will appear in the output. These statistics include the mean, standard deviation, and standard error for each condition. To compute other statistics (e.g., range or skewness), use the CONDESCRIPTIVE procedure described in Chapter 4.

PUTTING THE SPSS^x FILE TOGETHER

Assume that you studied the effects of parental involvement (independent variable) on students' grades (dependent variable). Half of the students in a

FIGURE 7.1   Data Sheet for Parental Involvement Experiment

STUDENT	PARENTAL INVOLVEMENT CONDITION[a]	FINAL GRADE AVERAGE
01	1	78.6
02	1	64.9
03	1	100.0
.	.	.
.	.	.
.	.	.
34	2	81.0
35	2	69.5
36	2	73.8

[a]Code for parental involvement condition: parental involvement = 1, no parental involvement = 2.

FIGURE 7.2   SPSS^x File for Parental Involvement Experiment

```
JOB. . .
EXEC SPSSX. . .                    (JCL commands for your computer system)
TITLE  "PARENTAL INVOLVEMENT STUDY"
DATA LIST  /INVOLVE 4 GRADE 6-10
VARIABLE LABELS  INVOLVE "PARENTAL INVOLVEMENT"
                 GRADE "FINAL GRADE AVERAGE"
VALUE LABELS  INVOLVE 1 "HIGH" 2 "LOW"
T-TEST  GROUPS=INVOLVE/VARIABLES=GRADE
BEGIN DATA
01 1  78.6
02 1  64.9
03 1 100.0
 .
 .
 .
34 2  81.0
35 2  69.5
36 2  73.8
END DATA
FINISH
END OF JOB  . . .                  (JCL command for your computer system)
```

third grade class were randomly assigned to the parental involvement group. The teacher contacted the parents of these children throughout the year and told them about the educational objectives of the class. Further, the teacher gave the parents specific methods for encouraging their children's educational activities. The other half of the students in the class were assigned to the no parental involvement group. At the end of the term, the average grades were tabulated for all of the children, and these are presented in Figure 7.1. Try to write an SPSS^x file that will allow you to determine whether parental involvement significantly influenced students' grades. When you have done this, check your SPSS^x file with the one that appears in Figure 7.2.

Notes and Variations

DATA LIST /INVOLVE 4 GRADE 6-10

> Given the way the numbers appear in the data lines, the preceding DATA LIST command is accurate. For the sake of clarity, we included the student numbers, blanks between the variables, and decimal points in the data lines. Do not feel constrained by this format. The important point is that, regardless of the format of your data lines, the column positions of your variables must be accurately specified in the DATA LIST command. For example, the data lines could have been typed in the following format:

```
(Columns 1...5)
        ↓   ↓
        1 786
        1 649
        11000
          .

          .

          .
        2 810
        2 695
        2 738
```

If you used this format, your DATA LIST command should look like the following one:

DATA LIST   /INVOLVE 1 GRADE 2-5 (1)

Recall that the (1) after GRADE 2-5 refers to the existence of one decimal place, although it is not literally typed on the data lines.

VARIABLE LABELS   INVOLVE "PARENTAL INVOLVEMENT"

This command causes the computer to write a longer label (up to 40 columns) for the variable on the printout. This is an optional command but is useful in clarifying the printout.

VALUE LABELS   INVOLVE 1 "HIGH" 2 "LOW"

This command causes the computer to list a more extensive description (up to 20 columns) of the levels of your independent variables on the printout. This command is optional also but aids greatly in the interpretation of the printout.

Note that the variables listed in the VARIABLE LABELS, VALUE LABELS, and T-TEST commands *must be spelled exactly* as they appear in the DATA LIST command.

The following examples should give you further practice in writing SPSSˣ files with the T-TEST procedure. In these examples, an experiment with two dependent variables is presented, the SAVE and the GET commands are used, and sample printouts and explanations of these printouts are given.

EXAMPLE 1: ALCOHOL AND REACTION TIME EXPERIMENT

Suppose that in order to test the effects of alcohol consumption (independent variable) on reaction time (dependent variable), eight subjects were assigned to each of two conditions. All 16 subjects were given six glasses of

FIGURE 7.3   Data Sheet for Reaction Time Experiment

SUBJECT NUMBER	ALCOHOL CONDITION[a]	VISUAL REACTION TIME (IN MSEC)	AUDITORY REACTION TIME (IN MSEC)
01	1	270	297
02	1	210	316
03	1	301	325
04	1	340	280
05	1	293	264
06	1	295	275
07	1	310	318
08	1	325	403
09	2	408	382
10	2	454	369
11	2	357	421
12	2	435	488
13	2	320	324
14	2	415	410
15	2	395	447
16	2	370	389

[a]Code for alcohol condition: placebo = 1, alcohol = 2.

a beverage to drink over a one-hour period. No alcohol was added to the glasses of the eight subjects in the placebo condition, and an ounce of tasteless alcohol was added to each of the glasses consumed by the eight subjects in the alcohol condition. After drinking their respective beverages, all subjects were tested on two reaction time tasks (two dependent variables): one with a visual stimulus (VISRT) and one with an auditory stimulus (AUDRT).

We wish to compare the alcohol and placebo conditions on both of the reaction time measures. Thus, two *t*-tests should be performed, one for each of the dependent measures. The data sheet for this experiment appears in Figure 7.3, and the SPSS[x] file for performing T-TEST is presented in Figure 7.4.

Output from the T-TEST Procedure

As shown in Figure 7.5, separate *t*-tests are performed for each dependent variable listed in the T-TEST command. Reading from left to right in the figure, the following statistics are listed:

1. The number of cases, mean, standard deviation, and the standard error for each group.
2. An *F* test, which is used to evaluate the basic assumption of the *t*-test that the variances of the two groups are approximately equal (homogeneity of variance). If the *F* value reported here is very high (and the probability value very

FIGURE 7.4   SPSSˣ File for the Reaction Time Experiment

```
JOB. . .
EXEC SPSSX. . .              (JCL commands for your computer system)
TITLE  "T-TEST FOR REACTION TIME EXPERIMENT"
FILE HANDLE  RT01/local system specifications
DATA LIST  /ALCOHOL 4 VISRT 6-8 AUDRT 10-12
VARIABLE LABELS  ALCOHOL "ALCOHOL CONDITION"
                 VISRT "REACTION TIME TO VISUAL STIMULUS"
                 AUDRT "REACTION TIME TO AUDITORY STIMULUS"
VALUE LABELS  ALCOHOL 1 "PLACEBO" 2 "ALCOHOL"
T-TEST  GROUPS=ALCOHOL/VARIABLES=VISRT AUDRT
BEGIN DATA
01 1 270 297
02 1 210 316
03 1 301 325
04 1 340 280
05 1 293 264
06 1 295 275
07 1 310 318
08 1 325 403
09 2 408 382
10 2 454 369
11 2 357 421
12 2 435 488
13 2 320 324
14 2 415 410
15 2 395 447
16 2 370 389
END DATA
SAVE  OUTFILE=RT01
FINISH
END OF JOB. . .             (JCL command for your computer system)
```

low—usually lower than .05 or .01), then the assumption of homogeneity of variance has been violated.

3. In most instances, the homogeneity of variance assumption *is* satisfied (as in the present example), and the traditional *t* value (using a *pooled variance estimate*) is used to evaluate the hypotheses.

4. When the assumption of homogeneity of variance *is not* satisfied, then the *t* value, which was computed using a *separate variance estimate* (located in the far right of the table), is used to evaluate the hypotheses.

In one case, you can see that 2-TAIL PROB is equal to 0.000; this means that the probability level is less than .001.

FIGURE 7.5 Output of T-TEST Procedure for Reaction Time Experiment

FIGURE 7.6   SPSSˣ File of Additional Analysis on Reaction Time Experiment

```
JOB. . .
EXEC SPSSX. . .                (JCL commands for your computer system)
TITLE "T-TEST FOR ADDITIONAL ANALYSIS"
FILE HANDLE  RT01/local system specifications
GET  FILE=RT01
COMPUTE  TOTRT=VISRT+AUDRT
VARIABLE LABELS  TOTRT "SUM OF VISUAL AND AUDITORY RTS"
T-TEST  GROUPS=ALCOHOL/VARIABLES=TOTRT
FINISH
END OF JOB. . .                (JCL command for your computer system)
```

EXAMPLE 2: REACTION TIME EXPERIMENT—ADDITIONAL ANALYSIS

Suppose that you want to perform one other analysis on the reaction time data. Specifically, you wish to examine the effects of alcohol on a combined reaction time, which represents the addition of the visual reaction time to the auditory reaction time. This can be done by using the COMPUTE command to create a new variable (TOTRT). Given that the data have been stored in system file RT01, the GET command can be used to run this analysis. An SPSSˣ file that performs the T-TEST procedure on the combined reaction time measure is presented in Figure 7.6, and the output is shown in Figure 7.7.

GENERAL CHARACTERISTICS AND LIMITATIONS OF THE T-TEST PROCEDURE

1. It is *not* necessary to have an equal number of cases or subjects in each group.
2. Each of the subcommands (VARIABLES= and GROUPS=) can appear only once on a given T-TEST command.
3. You are limited to the core storage space available to you on your computer system. If you exceed this limitation, you can reduce your core storage requirements by specifying fewer dependent variables in the T-TEST command and by using several T-TEST statements at the end of your data lines.

FIGURE 7.7 Output for Additional Analysis on Reaction Time Experiment

- - - - - - - - - - - - - - - - - - - T - T E S T - - - - - - - - - - - - - - - - - - -

GROUP 1 - ALCOHOL EQ 1.
GROUP 2 - ALCOHOL EQ 2.

VARIABLE	NUMBER OF CASES	MEAN	STANDARD DEVIATION	STANDARD ERROR		F VALUE	2-TAIL PROB.		POOLED VARIANCE ESTIMATE T VALUE	DEGREES OF FREEDOM	2-TAIL PROB.		SEPARATE VARIANCE ESTIMATE T VALUE	DEGREES OF FREEDOM	2-TAIL PROB.
TOTRT SUM OF VISUAL AND AUDITORY RTS.					*			*				*			
GROUP 1	8	602.7500	62.675	22.159	*	1.62	0.539	*	-5.44	14	0.000	*	-5.44	13.25	0.000
GROUP 2	8	798.0000	79.836	28.226	*			*				*			

T-TEST: Student's *t*-test for Within-Subjects Designs

PURPOSE

T-TEST is the SPSS^x procedure that computes Student's *t*-test. This test is used to examine the effects of one independent variable on one or more dependent variables and is restricted to comparisons of *two* conditions (two levels of the independent variable). The results of this test enable you to determine if two means differ significantly. Two basic experimental designs, between-subjects and within-subjects designs, can be analyzed with the T-TEST procedure. It is important to distinguish between these two types of designs because they require different statistical procedures and, consequently, different forms of the T-TEST command. In the previous chapter, we described how to use the T-TEST procedure for analyzing between-subjects designs, and in this chapter, we focus on how to analyze within-subjects designs.

In a within-subjects or repeated measures design, all participants are administered all levels of the independent variable. For example, assume that you are interested in examining the effects of two types of drugs (X,Y) on reaction time. Using a within-subjects design, you would expose all subjects to both levels of the drug variable; that is, each subject's reaction time would be tested while the subject was under the influence of one of the drugs *and* then later while under the influence of the other drug. In this design, all participants contribute two scores, which are treated as pairs. (To help clarify the difference between within- and between-subjects designs, you might want to contrast the preceding description with the description of a between-subjects design in the previous chapter.)

GENERAL FORMAT OF THE T-TEST COMMAND

The general format for the T-TEST procedure for within-subjects designs is

```
T-TEST  PAIRS=VAR1 VAR2
```

The preceding command causes a *t*-test to be performed that compares the mean of one level of the independent variable (VAR1) with the mean of the other level of the independent variable (VAR2). The levels (designated with variable names) that you wish to compare should be listed (separated by a blank) after the PAIRS= subcommand. For example, assume that you conducted an experiment, using a within-subjects design, to test the effects of sleep deprivation (four hours, eight hours) on reading speed. That is, all subjects participated in both the four-hour (HR4) and eight-hour (HR8) deprivation interval. In this case, the following format is appropriate:

```
T-TEST  PAIRS=HR4 HR8
```

VARIATIONS IN THE FORMAT OF THE T-TEST COMMAND

If there are more than two levels of the independent variable and you wish to perform all possible pairwise comparisons, then list all of the variable names (separated by blank spaces) after the PAIRS= subcommand. For example, suppose there were four levels of sleep deprivation (HR4, HR8, HR12, and HR16). The following command would cause all possible pairwise comparisons to be performed:

```
T-TEST  PAIRS=HR4 HR8 HR12 HR16
```

Here you are requesting six *t*-tests: HR4 with HR8, HR4 with HR12, HR4 with HR16, HR8 with HR12, HR8 with HR16, and HR12 with HR16.

The word WITH can also be used to set up specific pairwise comparisons. In the following example, three *t*-tests are requested (HR4 with HR8, HR4 with HR12, and HR4 with HR16).

```
T-TEST  PAIRS=HR4 WITH HR8 HR12 HR16
```

You may also request several sets of *t*-tests with a single T-TEST command—just use slashes to separate them.

```
T-TEST  PAIRS=HR4 WITH HR8 HR12 HR16/HR8 HR16
```

This command would result in four *t*-tests—HR4 with HR8, HR4 with HR12, HR4 with HR16, and HR8 with HR16.

Although you are unlikely to exceed this limitation, no more than 400 variables can be listed after the PAIRS= subcommand.

COMMONLY USED OPTIONS

Three OPTIONS are commonly used with the T-TEST procedure. You may include some or none of these in your SPSS˟ file. If you desire to invoke an option, then the OPTIONS command should follow the T-TEST command and the following format should be used.

```
OPTIONS  1
```

Causes all previous MISSING VALUES commands to be ignored. Therefore, *all* of the data would be included in the analysis—even those with codes representing missing data.

```
OPTIONS  2
```

Causes a case to be eliminated from the analysis entirely if that case contains missing data on any of the variables listed after the PAIRS= subcommand.

If this option is not included, then the *default option* for missing data is in effect. The default option causes a case or subject to be eliminated from the analysis if there is a missing value for either variable or if there are missing values for both variables of any particular analysis.

```
OPTIONS  4
```

Causes the computer to print the results within 80 columns.

If more than one option is desired, list the appropriate numbers, separated by spaces:

```
OPTIONS  1 4
```

If no options are desired, omit the OPTIONS command altogether.

STATISTICS

No optional statistics are available with the T-TEST procedure. (Thus you should not include a STATISTICS command.) In a normal run of the T-TEST procedure, several statistics will automatically be computed, and these will appear in the output. These statistics include the mean, standard

FIGURE 8.1 Data Sheet for Problem-Solving Experiment

SUBJECT NUMBER	ALONE	WITH OTHERS
01	12	10
02	8	6
03	4	4
.	.	.
.	.	.
.	.	.
12	5	2

deviation, and standard error for each condition. Additionally, the mean, variance, and standard deviation of the difference scores (the difference between each subject's scores in the two conditions) are listed in the printout. To compute other statistics (e.g., range or skewness), use the CONDESCRIPTIVE procedure described in Chapter 4.

PUTTING THE SPSSˣ FILE TOGETHER

Imagine that you conducted an experiment to test the effects of the presence of others (independent variable) on problem-solving performance (dependent variable). Assume also that you used a within-subjects design. That is, all 12 subjects in the experiment solved problems under both

FIGURE 8.2 SPSSˣ File for Problem-Solving Experiment

```
JOB. . .
EXEC SPSSX. . .              (JCL commands for your computer system)
TITLE  "EFFECTS OF OTHERS ON PERFORMANCE"
DATA LIST  /ALONE 4-5 OTHERS 7-8
VARIABLE LABELS  ALONE "PROBLEM SOLVING ALONE"
                 OTHERS "PROBLEM SOLVING WITH OTHERS"
T-TEST  PAIRS=ALONE OTHERS
BEGIN DATA
01 12 10
02  8  6
03  4  4
.

.

12  5  2
END DATA
FINISH
END OF JOB. . .            (JCL command for your computer system)
```

conditions of the independent variable (alone, in the presence of others). Subjects were tested in these two conditions on different days using comparable tasks, and the number of problems correctly solved was recorded. The data sheet for this experiment appears in Figure 8.1. Write an SPSS[x] file to determine if the presence of others has a reliable effect on problem-solving performance. After you have written your SPSS[x] file, compare it with the one shown in Figure 8.2.

Notes and Variations

DATA LIST   /ALONE 4–5 OTHERS 7–8

> This DATA LIST command accurately specifies the positions of the variable values on the data lines. There are, however, other formats that you could have used to type in your data. For maximum efficiency, you could have eliminated the subject numbers and omitted the blank spaces between the variables as shown:

```
(Columns 1 . . 4)
       ↓   ↓
      1210
       8 6
       4 4
       .
       .
       .
       5 2
```

> If you used this format, the DATA LIST statement should look like the following one.

DATA LIST   /ALONE 1–2 OTHERS 3–4

VARIABLE LABELS   ALONE "PROBLEM SOLVING ALONE"

> This command causes a more extensive label of the variable (up to 40 columns) to appear on the printout. This is an optional command.

Note that the variables listed in the VARIABLE LABELS and T-TEST commands *must be spelled exactly* as they appear in the DATA LIST command.

In addition to providing you with further practice in writing SPSS[x] files, the following examples demonstrate the uses of the SAVE and GET commands. Also, the printouts that result from a within-subjects T-TEST procedure are presented and explained.

EXAMPLE 1: ALCOHOL AND REACTION TIME EXPERIMENT

Assume that we tested the effects of alcohol consumption (independent variable) on reaction time (dependent variable) using a within-subjects design. Eight subjects received both levels of the independent variable on different days.

1. Alcohol—Subjects consumed six glasses of a beverage, and each glass contained one ounce of a tasteless alcoholic beverage.
2. Placebo—Subjects consumed six glasses of the same beverage without alcohol.

Two reaction time tests were used: one to a visual stimulus and one to an auditory stimulus (two dependent variables), and both reaction times were recorded for each independent variable condition (PVISRT, PAUDRT, AVISRT, AAUDRT).

We wish to examine the effects of alcohol for both visual and auditory reaction time measures. To do this, two *t*-tests need to be performed, one for each of the two reaction time measures. The data sheet for this experiment is presented in Figure 8.3, and an SPSS^x file that contains the commands for performing the preceding analyses is presented in Figure 8.4.

Output from the T-TEST Procedure

The printout from the T-TEST procedure is presented in Figure 8.5. As shown, a separate table is printed for each *t*-test requested and various statistics have been calculated. These include

1. The number of cases or subjects, mean, standard deviation, and standard error for each condition or level of the independent variable
2. The mean, standard deviation, and standard error of the difference scores

FIGURE 8.3   Data Sheet for Reaction Time Experiment

	PLACEBO		ALCOHOL	
SUBJECT NUMBER	VISUAL REACTION TIME	AUDITORY REACTION TIME	VISUAL REACTION TIME	AUDITORY REACTION TIME
01	270	264	408	410
02	210	280	454	447
03	301	316	357	382
04	340	325	435	421
05	293	275	320	369
06	295	297	415	488
07	310	403	395	324
08	325	318	370	389

FIGURE 8.4   SPSSˣ File for Reaction Time Experiment

```
JOB. . .
EXEC SPSSX. . .                 (JCL commands for your computer system)
TITLE  "T-TEST FOR REACTION TIME EXPERIMENT"
FILE HANDLE  RT02/local system specifications
DATA LIST  /PVISRT 4-6 PAUDRT 8-10 AVISRT 12-14 AAUDRT 16-18
VARIABLE LABELS  PVISRT "PLACEBO VISUAL REACTION TIME"
                 PAUDRT "PLACEBO AUDITORY REACTION TIME"
                 AVISRT "ALCOHOL VISUAL REACTION TIME"
                 AAUDRT "ALCOHOL AUDITORY REACTION TIME"
T-TEST  PAIRS=PVISRT AVISRT/PAUDRT AAUDRT
BEGIN DATA
01 270 264 408 410
02 210 280 454 447
03 301 316 357 382
04 340 325 435 421
05 293 275 320 369
06 295 297 415 488
07 310 403 395 324
08 325 318 370 389
END DATA
SAVE  OUTFILE=RT02
FINISH
END OF JOB. . .                 (JCL command for your computer system)
```

      (i.e., the difference between each subject's scores under the two levels of the independent variable)

3. The Pearson product-moment correlation coefficient (and the level of significance), which is computed between the two levels of the independent variable

4. The value of *t*, degrees of freedom, and significance level for the within-subjects *t*-test

Note that in some cases the 2-TAIL PROB may be equal to 0.000. This means that the probability of chance is *less than* .001.

EXAMPLE 2: REACTION TIME EXPERIMENT—ADDITIONAL ANALYSIS

Assume that you now want to perform an additional *t*-test. You wish to compare the alcohol and placebo conditions on a total reaction time score, one that combines the visual and auditory reaction times. The COMPUTE command can be used to create the combined reaction times scores

FIGURE 8.5 Output of T-TEST Procedure for Reaction Time Experiment

- T - T E S T -

VARIABLE	NUMBER OF CASES	MEAN	STANDARD DEVIATION	STANDARD ERROR	*(DIFFERENCE) MEAN	STANDARD DEVIATION	STANDARD ERROR	* CORR.	2-TAIL PROB. *	T VALUE	DEGREES OF FREEDOM	2-TAIL PROB.
PVISRT PLACEBO VISUAL REACTION TIME		293.0000	39.656	14.020								
	8				-101.2500	68.772	24.315	-0.361	0.379	-4.16	7	0.004
AVISRT ALCOHOL VISUAL REACTION TIME		394.2500	43.654	15.434								
PAUDRT PLACEBO AUDITORY REACTION TIME		309.7500	43.726	15.459								
	8				-94.0000	83.399	29.486	-0.579	0.133	-3.19	7	0.015
AAUDRT ALCOHOL AUDITORY REACTION TIME		403.7500	50.091	17.710								

FIGURE 8.6 SPSS^x File of Additional Analysis on Reaction Time Experiment

```
JOB. . .
EXEC SPSSX. . .                    (JCL commands for your computer system)
TITLE  "T-TEST FOR ADDITIONAL ANALYSIS"
FILE HANDLE  RT02/local system specifications
GET  FILE=RT02
COMPUTE  TOTPLA=PVISRT+PAUDRT
COMPUTE  TOTALC=AVISRT+AAUDRT
VARIABLE LABELS  TOTPLA "COMBINED RTS FOR PLACEBO GROUP"
                 TOTALC "COMBINED RTS FOR ALCOHOL GROUP"
T-TEST  PAIRS=TOTPLA TOTALC
FINISH
END OF JOB. . .                    (JCL command for your computer system)
```

(TOTPLA and TOTALC). Also, because the file RT02 was saved in the first analysis, the GET command can be used to access the data. Your SPSS^x file might look like the one in Figure 8.6, and the output is shown in Figure 8.7.

GENERAL CHARACTERISTICS AND LIMITATIONS OF THE T-TEST PROCEDURE

1. No more than 400 variables can be listed after the PAIRS= subcommand.
2. The PAIRS= subcommand can appear only once on a given T-TEST command.
3. You are limited to the core storage space available to you on your computer system. If you exceed this limitation, you can reduce your core storage requirements by using several T-TEST statements at the end of your data lines.

FIGURE 8.7 Output for Additional Analysis on Reaction Time Experiment

- T - T E S T -

VARIABLE	NUMBER OF CASES	MEAN	STANDARD DEVIATION	STANDARD ERROR	*(DIFFERENCE) MEAN	STANDARD DEVIATION	STANDARD ERROR	* 2-TAIL * CORR. PROB. *	T VALUE	DEGREES OF FREEDOM	2-TAIL PROB.
TOTPLA COMBINED RTS FOR PLACEBO GROUP											
	8	602.7500	72.324	25.570	-195.2500	131.375	46.448	-0.423 0.296	-4.20	7	0.004
TOTALC COMBINED RTS FOR ALCOHOL GROUP											
	8	798.0000	83.257	29.436							

109

ONEWAY: Analysis of Variance for One Independent Variable Designs

PURPOSE

The SPSS[x] procedure ONEWAY computes the analysis of variance for *between-subjects designs* that contain only *one* independent variable (i.e., designs in which subjects have been randomly assigned to two or more levels of one independent variable). ONEWAY is used to determine if two or more group means differ significantly. In the case of two group designs, it yields the same probability level as the T-TEST procedure. An *F* ratio is the statistic that is calculated by ONEWAY, and a significant *F* indicates that at least two group means differ. To determine specifically which groups differ from each other, further analyses are necessary, and the commands for several of these analyses are described later in this chapter.

GENERAL FORMAT AND VARIATIONS OF THE ONEWAY COMMAND

The general format for the ONEWAY procedure is

$$\text{ONEWAY} \quad \begin{matrix} \text{dependent} \\ \text{variable} \end{matrix} \quad \text{BY} \quad \begin{matrix} \text{independent} \\ \text{variable} \end{matrix} \quad \left(\begin{matrix} \text{minimum} & \text{maximum} \\ \text{value} & , & \text{value} \end{matrix} \right)$$

After the command ONEWAY, type the name of the dependent variable, then the word BY, then the name of the independent variable, and finally the minimum and maximum values of the independent variable. You should notice that the minimum and maximum values must be separated by a comma and enclosed within parentheses. Minimum and maximum values refer to the lowest and highest values or levels of the independent variable that you wish to include in your analysis. For example, three dosage values or levels of an independent variable called DRUG (levels 1, 2, and 3) might be coded as DRUG (1,3) as shown:

```
ONEWAY  DEPVAR BY DRUG (1,3)
```

This command requests that an analysis of variance be performed comparing all three levels of the independent variable called DRUG. With this format, it is assumed that values of 1, 2, or 3 have been typed on the data lines to identify the treatment condition of each subject.

If, for some reason, you wanted to exclude treatment condition 1 from the analysis and compare only conditions 2 and 3, you could use the following command:

```
ONEWAY  DEPVAR BY DRUG (2,3)
```

One restriction that you should be aware of is that the minimum and maximum values or levels of your independent variable must be numeric. If you wished to compare the performance of four brands of tires (Brands A, B, C, and D), you could *not* specify BRANDS (A,D) in your ONEWAY command. Thus, it would be wise to use numeric codes in your data lines. Otherwise, you would have to recode these alphanumeric values or levels (with the RECODE command) into numeric values (e.g., 1, 2, 3, and 4).

To perform several ONEWAY analyses (each one on a different dependent variable), you may include several ONEWAY procedure commands in the file, or you may use one of the following formats:

```
ONEWAY DEPVARA DEPVARB DEPVARC DEPVARD BY  independent (minimum  maximum)
                                            variable   ( value  ,  value )
```

or

```
ONEWAY  DEPVARA TO DEPVARD BY  independent (minimum   maximum)
                                variable   ( value  ,  value )
```

As an example, assume that four groups of children were shown one of four films that differed in terms of degree of violence depicted (independent variable). Then a behavioral measure of their subsequent aggression (dependent variable) was recorded. An appropriate ONEWAY procedure command is:

```
ONEWAY  AGGRESS BY VIOLENCE (1,4)
```

If the experimenter had collected three dependent measures (ACT1, ACT2, ACT3), appropriate formats would be

```
ONEWAY  ACT1 BY VIOLENCE (1,4)        Note that the first ONEWAY command
ONEWAY  ACT2 BY VIOLENCE (1,4)        should precede the BEGIN DATA line.
ONEWAY  ACT3 BY VIOLENCE (1,4)        The others go after the END DATA line.
```

or

```
ONEWAY  ACT1 ACT2 ACT3 BY VIOLENCE (1,4)
```

or

```
ONEWAY  ACT1 TO ACT3 BY VIOLENCE (1,4)
```

As another example, suppose that we tested the effects of sensory isolation (independent variable) on problem solving (dependent variable). Volunteers were randomly assigned to each of three sensory isolation conditions: 0 hours, 6 hours, and 12 hours. After isolation, all of the participants were given a problem-solving test. An appropriate ONEWAY procedure is

```
ONEWAY  PROBSOL BY SENISO (1,3)
```

If, in the preceding example, participants had been given five tests of performance (five dependent measures: TEST1, TEST2, TEST3, TEST4, and TEST5), any of the following formats would be appropriate:

```
ONEWAY  TEST1 BY SENISO (1,3)
ONEWAY  TEST2 BY SENISO (1,3)        Note that these additional
ONEWAY  TEST3 BY SENISO (1,3)        procedure commands would follow
ONEWAY  TEST4 BY SENISO (1,3)        the END DATA line.
ONEWAY  TEST5 BY SENISO (1,3)
```

or

```
ONEWAY  TEST1 TEST2 TEST3 TEST4 TEST5 BY SENISO (1,3)
```

or

```
ONEWAY  TEST1 TO TEST5 BY SENISO (1,3)
```

COMMONLY USED OPTIONS

Eight OPTIONS are available with the ONEWAY procedure. You may use some or none of these options in your program. Three are described here, and the rest can be found in the ONEWAY chapter of the *SPSS*[x] *User's Guide*. The OPTIONS command, if used, follows the ONEWAY command.

```
OPTIONS  1
```

Causes all previous MISSING VALUES commands to be ignored. Therefore, *all* of the data would be included in the analysis—even those with codes representing missing data.

OPTIONS 2

> Causes a case to be eliminated from *all* analyses listed on the
> ONEWAY command if that case contains missing data on *any*
> of the dependent measures listed on the ONEWAY command.

> If neither of these options is included, a participant's missing
> score on a particular measure is excluded *only from the analysis
> involving that measure.* Valid scores that the subject has on other
> measures will be included in the appropriate analyses. For
> example, if a subject has missing data on dependent variable *A*
> but not on dependent variables *B* and *C,* that subject or case
> will be eliminated only from the analysis involving dependent
> variable *A.*

OPTIONS 6

> Causes the first eight characters of the value labels for the
> levels of the independent variable to be printed out rather than
> the default labels, which are GRP1, GRP2, GRP3, . . . Because
> these labels enhance the readability of your printout, we
> suggest that you use this option.

If you desire more than one option, list the appropriate numbers,
separated by spaces:

OPTIONS 1 6

You may omit the OPTIONS command altogether if you do not wish to use
any of the possible options.

COMMONLY USED STATISTICS

Of the three STATISTICS available with the ONEWAY procedure, the
most commonly used is described subsequently. For other STATISTICS
dealing with homogeneity of variance and comparisons of fixed and random models, see the ONEWAY chapter in the *SPSS^x User's Guide.* The
STATISTICS command, if used, follows the OPTIONS command.

STATISTICS 1

> Causes the number of subjects, means, standard deviations,
> minimum and maximum scores, and the 95 percent confidence
> interval to be printed out for each group. These descriptive
> statistics are essential for interpreting and reporting your
> results, and thus, we strongly recommend that you request
> STATISTICS 1.

PUTTING THE SPSS^x FILE TOGETHER

As an educational researcher, assume that you conducted an experiment to
test whether preparation courses (independent variable) affect Scholastic

FIGURE 9.1   Data Sheet for SAT Experiment

STUDENT	STUDY CONDITION[a]	SAT SCORE
01	1	870
02	1	860
.	.	.
.	.	.
.	.	.
20	1	1020
21	2	1050
22	2	1070
.	.	.
.	.	.
.	.	.
40	2	880
41	3	1120
42	3	930
.	.	.
.	.	.
.	.	.
60	3	1090

[a]Code for study condition: 0 hours = 1, 20 hours = 2, 40 hours = 3.

Aptitude Test (SAT) performance (dependent variable). Specifically, 20 high school juniors were randomly assigned to each of three study conditions:

1. 0 hours of course work designed to prepare students for the SAT
2. 20 hours of course work designed to prepare students for the SAT
3. 40 hours of course work designed to prepare students for the SAT

After all the course work was completed, all 60 students were given the Scholastic Aptitude Test, and their scores are listed in Figure 9.1. Using these data, write an SPSS[x] file to determine if the three groups differed in terms of SAT performance. When you finish writing your SPSS[x] file, compare it with the one in Figure 9.2.

Notes and Variations

DATA LIST   /STUDY 4 SAT 6-9

As written, this command accurately specifies the locations of the variable values in the data lines. Note, however, that there are other possible formats for typing in your data. For maximum efficiency, you could have omitted the student numbers and the blank spaces between the variable values. Thus, if the data lines were typed in the following format

```
(Columns 1...5)
        ↓   ↓
        1 870
        1 860
        .
        .
        .
        11020
        21050
        21070
        .
        .
        .
        2 880
        31120
        3 930
        .
        .
        .
        31090
```

the DATA LIST statement should look like the following one.

```
DATA LIST   /STUDY 1 SAT 2-5
```

VARIABLES LABELS STUDY "STUDY CONDITION"

This causes a more extensive label of the variable (up to 40 columns) to appear on the printout. This is an optional command and is used to clarify the printout.

VALUE LABELS STUDY 1 "0 HOURS" 2 "20 HOURS" 3 "40 HOURS"

This statement, along with the OPTIONS 6 statement, causes the first eight characters of the labels for the levels of your independent variable to be printed in the output. Thus, in this case, the labels 0 HOURS, 20 HOURS, and 40 HOURS would appear in the printout. The VALUE LABELS and OPTIONS 6 statements are optional; however, the default labels are GRP1, GRP2, and GRP3, and these are not very descriptive.

STATISTICS 1

This optional command causes several statistics, including the means and standard deviations, to be calculated for each group.

Note that the variables listed in the VARIABLE LABELS, VALUE LABELS, and ONE-WAY commands *must be spelled exactly* as they appear in the DATA LIST statement.

The following examples should give you further practice in writing SPSS^x files. In these examples, an experiment with two dependent vari-

FIGURE 9.2   SPSS˟ File for SAT Experiment

```
JOB. . .
EXEC SPSSX. . .                    (JCL commands for your computer system)
TITLE  "EFFECTS OF PREPARATION ON SAT SCORES"
DATA LIST  /STUDY 4 SAT 6-9
VARIABLE LABELS  STUDY "STUDY CONDITION"
                 SAT "SCHOLASTIC APTITUDE SCORE"
VALUE LABELS  STUDY 1 "0 HOURS" 2 "20 HOURS" 3 "40 HOURS"
ONEWAY  SAT BY STUDY (1,3)
OPTIONS  6
STATISTICS  1
BEGIN DATA
01 1   870
02 1   860
 .
 .
 .
20 1  1020
21 2  1050
22 2  1070
 .
 .
 .
40 2   880
41 3  1120
42 3   930
 .
 .
 .
60 3  1090
END DATA
FINISH
END OF JOB. . .                    (JCL command for your computer system)
```

---

ables is presented, SAVE and GET commands are used, and sample printouts and explanations of these printouts are presented. Also, related analyses that are often performed with the ONEWAY procedure are described and demonstrated.

EXAMPLE 1: PROCESSING STRATEGIES EXPERIMENT

In an investigation of the effectiveness of different cognitive processing strategies (independent variable) on memory performance (dependent variable), 12 participants were randomly assigned to each of four learning conditions. They all learned the same list of words. The four processing strategies imposed on the groups were:

1. Use of imagery
2. Use of organization
3. Use of rhyme
4. Use of rote repetition

After the list was processed, a recall test and a recognition test were given to each of the subjects. In the experiment two dependent variables (recall and recognition) were recorded.

We wish to perform two separate analyses that will enable us to determine whether the four groups differ (1) in the recall measure and (2) in the recognition measure. The data sheet for this experiment is presented in Figure 9.3, and the SPSS^x file for performing ONEWAY is presented in Figure 9.4.

Output from the ONEWAY Procedure

As can be seen in Figure 9.5, the ONEWAY procedure statement causes an analysis of variance table to be printed for each dependent vari-

FIGURE 9.3 **Data Sheet for Processing Strategies Experiment**

SUBJECT NUMBER	GROUP[a]	RECALL SCORE	RECOGNITION SCORE
01	1	24	36
02	1	22	34
.	.	.	.
.	.	.	.
.	.	.	.
12	1	18	33
13	2	20	35
14	2	21	36
.	.	.	.
.	.	.	.
.	.	.	.
24	2	24	34
25	3	11	26
26	3	08	27
.	.	.	.
.	.	.	.
.	.	.	.
36	3	06	22
37	4	07	20
38	4	12	24
.	.	.	.
.	.	.	.
.	.	.	.
48	4	10	28

[a]Code for groups: imagery = 1, organization = 2, rhyme = 3, rote repetition = 4.

FIGURE 9.4   SPSSˣ File for the Processing Strategies Experiment

```
JOB. . .
EXEC SPSSX. . .                    (JCL commands for your computer)
TITLE  "ANALYSES OF VARIANCE FOR PROCESSING STRATEGIES EXPERIMENT"
FILE HANDLE  LEARN01/local system specifications
DATA LIST  /STRATEGY 4 RECALL 6-7 RECOG 9-10
VARIABLE LABELS  STRATEGY "PROCESSING STRATEGIES"
                 RECALL "NUMBER OF WORDS CORRECTLY RECALLED"
                 RECOG "NUMBER OF WORDS CORRECTLY RECOGNIZED"
VALUE LABELS  STRATEGY 1 "IMAGERY" 2 "ORGANIZATION" 3 "RHYME"
              4 "ROTE REPETITION"
ONEWAY  RECALL RECOG BY STRATEGY (1,4)
OPTIONS  6
STATISTICS  1
BEGIN DATA
01 1 24 36
02 1 22 34
 .
 .
 .
12 1 18 33
13 2 20 35
14 2 21 36
 .
 .
 .
24 2 24 34
25 3 11 26
26 3  8 27
 .
 .
 .
36 3  6 22
37 4  7 20
38 4 12 24
 .
 .
 .
48 4 10 28
END DATA
SAVE  OUTFILE=LEARN01
FINISH
END OF JOB. . .                    (JCL command for your computer system)
```

able. This table includes the source of variation, degrees of freedom, sum of squares, mean squares, F-ratio, and the probability level of the F-ratio (the probability that it was obtained on the basis of chance). In this output, you will notice that F PROB is equal to 0.000; this means that the probability level is *less than* .001. The output that results from the STATISTICS 1

FIGURE 9.5   Output for Processing Strategies Experiment

```
- - - - - - - - - - - - - - - - - - - - - - - - - - - - - O N E W A Y - - - - - - - - - - - - - - - - - -

    VARIABLE  RECALL      NUMBER OF WORDS CORRECTLY RECALLED
  BY VARIABLE STRATEGY    PROCESSING STRATEGIES

                                 ANALYSIS OF VARIANCE
```

SOURCE	D.F.	SUM OF SQUARES	MEAN SQUARES	F RATIO	F PROB.
BETWEEN GROUPS	3	1675.5833	558.5278	41.2567	.0000
WITHIN GROUPS	44	595.6667	13.5379		
TOTAL	47	2271.2500			

GROUP	COUNT	MEAN	STANDARD DEVIATION	STANDARD ERROR	MINIMUM	MAXIMUM	95 PCT CONF INT FOR MEAN	
IMAGERY	12	20.8333	3.6639	1.0577	15.0000	28.0000	18.5054 TO	23.1613
ORGANIZA	12	22.1667	2.9181	.8424	17.0000	27.0000	20.3126 TO	24.0207
RHYME	12	10.3333	3.8218	1.1033	4.0000	17.0000	7.9051 TO	12.7616
ROTE REP	12	9.1667	4.1960	1.2113	1.0000	15.0000	6.5007 TO	11.8327
TOTALREP	48	15.6250	6.9516	1.0034	1.0000	28.0000	13.6065 TO	17.6435

```
- - - - - - - - - - - - - - - - - - - - - - - - - - - - - O N E W A Y - - - - - - - - - - - - - - - - - -

    VARIABLE  RECOG       NUMBER OF WORDS CORRECTLY RECOGNIZED
  BY VARIABLE STRATEGY    PROCESSING STRATEGIES

                                 ANALYSIS OF VARIANCE
```

SOURCE	D.F.	SUM OF SQUARES	MEAN SQUARES	F RATIO	F PROB.
BETWEEN GROUPS	3	1288.0625	429.3542	32.5203	.0000
WITHIN GROUPS	44	580.9167	13.2027		
TOTAL	47	1868.9792			

GROUP	COUNT	MEAN	STANDARD DEVIATION	STANDARD ERROR	MINIMUM	MAXIMUM	95 PCT CONF INT FOR MEAN	
IMAGERY	12	32.3333	3.1140	.8989	26.0000	36.0000	30.3548 TO	34.3119
ORGANIZA	12	30.6667	3.4728	1.0025	26.0000	36.0000	28.4601 TO	32.8732
RHYME	12	21.3333	4.4992	1.2988	14.0000	29.0000	18.4747 TO	24.1920
ROTE REP	12	21.0833	3.2879	.9491	14.0000	26.0000	18.9943 TO	23.1724
TOTALREP	48	26.3542	6.3060	.9102	14.0000	36.0000	24.5231 TO	28.1852

statement is also presented in Figure 9.5. This statement leads to the printout of the number of subjects or cases per group, means, standard deviations, standard errors, minimum and maximum scores, and the 95 percent confidence intervals for the mean of each group. Note here the effect of the OPTIONS 6 statement: the labels IMAGERY, ORGANIZA, RHYME, and ROTE REP appear in the printout rather than the default labels GRP1, GRP2, GRP3, and GRP4.

RELATED ANALYSES

As mentioned previously, the ONEWAY procedure causes an *F*-ratio to be computed. A significant *F* allows you to conclude that your group means are not equal (i.e., that at least one difference exists among your groups). With two group designs, this result is straightforward and tells you that the mean of Group 1 is significantly different from that of Group 2. With more

FIGURE 9.6   A Posteriori Tests Available with ONEWAY

TEST	SPSS˟ NAME	POSSIBLE ALPHA LEVELS
Least Significant Difference	LSD	Any alpha
Duncan's Multiple Range	DUNCAN	.10, .05, .01
Student-Newman-Keuls	SNK	.05
Tukey's Alternative Procedure	TUKEYB	.05
Honestly Significant Difference	TUKEY	.05
Modified Least Significant Difference	LSDMOD	Any alpha
Scheffe's	SCHEFFE	Any alpha

than two groups, however, a significant F does not tell you *which* groups differ significantly. For example, Group 1 may differ from Groups 2 and 3 and Groups 2 and 3 may not differ from each other, or Group 1 may differ from Group 2 and Group 2 may differ from Group 3, and so on. To determine which group means differ significantly, several statistical tests are available with ONEWAY. The tests to be described here are generally known as a posteriori (or post hoc) tests, and they are used when comparisons or contrasts have not been specified in advance (i.e., you have not planned—on the basis of your hypotheses—to compare specific group means). These tests yield all possible pairwise comparisons between the group means in your experiment. The different a posteriori statistical tests available with the ONEWAY procedure are listed in Figure 9.6.

Any or all of these a posteriori tests can be applied to your data by using the subcommand RANGES. The general format for performing one or more of these tests with ONEWAY is

$$\text{ONEWAY} \quad \begin{array}{c} \text{dependent} \\ \text{variable} \end{array} \text{BY} \begin{array}{c} \text{independent} \\ \text{variable} \end{array} \left(\begin{array}{c} \text{minimum} \\ \text{value} \end{array} , \begin{array}{c} \text{maximum} \\ \text{value} \end{array} \right) \Big/$$

$$\text{RANGES} \quad = \quad \text{test name (alpha level)}$$

Notice that the ONEWAY specifications must be separated from the RANGES subcommand by a slash. The alpha level specification is optional, and if the alpha level is not specified, the default value of .05 will be assumed. Also, *no more than 10 RANGES commands* can appear with each ONEWAY command.

As an example, assume that we wish to compare all possible pairs of means in the processing strategies experiment using the Least Significant Difference Test (alpha = .01), Duncan's Multiple Range Test (alpha = .05), and the Honestly Significant Difference Test (alpha = .05). The following statements would cause SPSS˟ to perform these comparisons:

```
ONEWAY  RECALL RECOG BY STRATEGY (1,4)/
        RANGES=LSD (01)/
        RANGES=DUNCAN/
        RANGES=TUKEY
```

FIGURE 9.7   Output of RANGES Commands for Processing Strategies Experiment

```
- - - - - - - - - - - - - - - - - - - - - - - - - - - - - - - - O N E W A Y - - - - - - - -


        VARIABLE  RECALL     NUMBER OF WORDS CORRECTLY RECALLED
     BY VARIABLE  STRATEGY   PROCESSING STRATEGIES


MULTIPLE RANGE TEST


LSD PROCEDURE
RANGES FOR THE 0.010 LEVEL -

        3.81    3.81    3.81

THE RANGES ABOVE ARE TABLE RANGES.
THE VALUE ACTUALLY COMPARED WITH MEAN(J)-MEAN(I) IS..
        2.6017 * RANGE * DSQRT(1/N(I) + 1/N(J))


   (*) DENOTES PAIRS OF GROUPS SIGNIFICANTLY DIFFERENT AT THE 0.010 LEVEL


                              R R I O
                              O H M R
                              T Y A G
                              E M G A
                                E E N
                              R   R I
                              E   Y Z
        MEAN       GROUP      P     A

        9.1667    ROTE REP
       10.3333    RHYME
       20.8333    IMAGERY    * *
       22.1667    ORGANIZA   * *


   HOMOGENEOUS SUBSETS   (SUBSETS OF GROUPS, WHOSE HIGHEST AND LOWEST MEANS
                          DO NOT DIFFER BY MORE THAN THE SHORTEST
                          SIGNIFICANT RANGE FOR A SUBSET OF THAT SIZE)


SUBSET   1

GROUP        ROTE REP      RHYME
MEAN          9.1667      10.3333
- - - - - - - - - - - - - - - - -


SUBSET   2

GROUP        IMAGERY      ORGANIZA
MEAN         20.8333       22.1667
- - - - - - - - - - - - - - - - -



        VARIABLE  RECALL     NUMBER OF WORDS CORRECTLY RECALLED
     BY VARIABLE  STRATEGY   PROCESSING STRATEGIES


MULTIPLE RANGE TEST


DUNCAN PROCEDURE
RANGES FOR THE 0.050 LEVEL -

        2.85    3.00    3.10

THE RANGES ABOVE ARE TABLE RANGES.
THE VALUE ACTUALLY COMPARED WITH MEAN(J)-MEAN(I) IS..
        2.6017 * RANGE * DSQRT(1/N(I) + 1/N(J))


   (*) DENOTES PAIRS OF GROUPS SIGNIFICANTLY DIFFERENT AT THE 0.050 LEVEL


                              R R I O
                              O H M R
                              T Y A G
                              E M G A
                                E E N
                              R   R I
                              E   Y Z
        MEAN       GROUP      P     A

        9.1667    ROTE REP
       10.3333    RHYME
       20.8333    IMAGERY    * *
       22.1667    ORGANIZA   * *
```

continued

FIGURE 9.7 *(Continued)*

```
HOMOGENEOUS SUBSETS    (SUBSETS OF GROUPS, WHOSE HIGHEST AND LOWEST MEANS
                        DO NOT DIFFER BY MORE THAN THE SHORTEST
                        SIGNIFICANT RANGE FOR A SUBSET OF THAT SIZE)

SUBSET  1

'GROUP         ROTE REP       RHYME
MEAN           9.1667        10.3333
- - - - - - - - - - - - - - - - -


SUBSET  2

GROUP          IMAGERY        ORGANIZA
MEAN           20.8333        22.1667
- - - - - - - - - - - - - - - - -


        VARIABLE  RECALL      NUMBER OF WORDS CORRECTLY RECALLED
     BY VARIABLE  STRATEGY    PROCESSING STRATEGIES


MULTIPLE RANGE TEST


TUKEY-HSD PROCEDURE
RANGES FOR THE 0.050 LEVEL -

        3.77    3.77    3.77

THE RANGES ABOVE ARE TABLE RANGES.
THE VALUE ACTUALLY COMPARED WITH MEAN(J)-MEAN(I) IS..
     2.6017 * RANGE * DSQRT(1/N(I) + 1/N(J))


 (*) DENOTES PAIRS OF GROUPS SIGNIFICANTLY DIFFERENT AT THE 0.050 LEVEL


                          R R I O
                          O H M R
                          T Y A G
                          E M G A
                            E E N
                          R   R I
                          E   Y Z
            MEAN   GROUP  P     A

          9.1667  ROTE REP
         10.3333  RHYME
         20.8333  IMAGERY   * *
         22.1667  ORGANIZA  * *

    HOMOGENEOUS SUBSETS    (SUBSETS OF GROUPS, WHOSE HIGHEST AND LOWEST MEANS
                            DO NOT DIFFER BY MORE THAN THE SHORTEST
                            SIGNIFICANT RANGE FOR A SUBSET OF THAT SIZE)


SUBSET  1

'GROUP         ROTE REP       RHYME
MEAN           9.1667        10.3333
- - - - - - - - - - - - - - - - -


SUBSET  2

GROUP          IMAGERY        ORGANIZA
MEAN           20.8333        22.1667
- - - - - - - - - - - - - - - - -
```

The output from the preceding RANGES commands is presented in Figure 9.7. Each a posteriori test that you requested has a heading that includes the dependent variable, the name of the test, and the alpha level that you selected. Note that the default alpha level (.05) was used for the Duncan and Tukey tests. In most situations, each RANGES command will provide you with two methods for interpreting the results of your a posteriori tests. First, you will be presented with a matrix in which each group is represented both horizontally and vertically. Asterisks (*) in the columns signify significant differences between the corresponding group means. For example, in the first matrix in Figure 9.7, the asterisks indicate that the mean of the ROTE REP group differs reliably from the means of the IMAGERY and ORGANIZA groups. Similarly, the mean of the RHYME group differs significantly from the means of the IMAGERY and ORGANIZA groups. The absence of asterisks in the other columns denotes that the means of the ROTE REP and RHYME groups do not differ from each other and that there is no reliable difference between the means of the IMAGERY and ORGANIZA groups.

Most of the time the RANGES command will also provide you with a subset analysis of your means (which yields the same conclusions as the matrix analysis). For the subset analysis, group means that appear in the same subset do not differ reliably. As can be seen in the printout, ROTE REP and RHYME appear together in Subset 1; this indicates that these two group means do not differ significantly. Likewise, the result that IMAGERY and ORGANIZA occur together in Subset 2 reveals that these two group means do not differ significantly. One can conclude that the means of the ROTE REP and RHYME groups are significantly lower than the means of the IMAGERY and ORGANIZA groups because these two sets of groups never appear together in the same subset. For further description of the a posteriori tests and descriptions of a priori comparisons (using the subcommand CONTRAST) and trend analyses (using the subcommand POLYNOMIAL), consult the *SPSS^x User's Guide.*

EXAMPLE 2: PROCESSING STRATEGIES EXPERIMENT—
ADDITIONAL ANALYSES

Assume that we wish to run additional analyses on the data from the processing strategies experiment. We wish to do the following:

1. Exclude the rote repetition group from the analyses
2. Eliminate subjects who recalled fewer than seven words from the recall analysis
3. Eliminate subjects who recognized fewer than 15 items from the recognition analysis
4. Run Duncan's Multiple Range Test to make all possible pairwise comparisons using the alpha levels of .05 and .01

Because the data from the previous analyses have been saved in an SPSS^x system file LEARN01, the GET command can be used to run these additional analyses. An example of an SPSS^x file that contains the statements necessary to perform the desired analyses is presented in Figure 9.8.

Notice that a TEMPORARY statement preceding the first SELECT

FIGURE 9.8   SPSS^x File of Additional Analyses on Processing Strategies Experiment

```
JOB. . .
EXEC SPSSX. . .              (JCL commands for your computer system)
TITLE "ONEWAY FOR ADDTIONAL ANALYSES"
FILE HANDLE  LEARN01/local system specifications
GET  FILE=LEARN01
TEMPORARY
SELECT IF  (RECALL GE 7)
ONEWAY  RECALL BY STRATEGY (1,3)/
        RANGES=DUNCAN/
        RANGES=DUNCAN (.01)
OPTIONS  6
STATISTICS  1
SELECT IF  (RECOG GE 15)
ONEWAY  RECOG BY STRATEGY (1,3)/
        RANGES=DUNCAN/
        RANGES=DUNCAN (.01)
OPTIONS  6
STATISTICS  1
FINISH
END OF JOB. . .             (JCL command for your computer system)
```

IF statement causes that selection to apply only to the procedure immediately following it. Subjects who recalled fewer than seven items would be excluded from the ONEWAY RECALL BY STRATEGY (1,3) analysis but not from the ONEWAY RECOG BY STRATEGY (1,3) analysis. Notice also that the rote repetition group was eliminated by changing the maximum value from 4 to 3 for the independent variable STRATEGY in the ONEWAY procedure commands.

A partial printout—for the analysis of the recall measure and for the first RANGES=DUNCAN/ statement—appears in Figure 9.9. Because no alpha level was specified in the command, the default alpha level of .05 was used. As shown in the bottom portion of the figure, there are asterisks under the RHYME column next to the IMAGERY and ORGANIZA groups, and the IMAGERY and ORGANIZA groups do not share any asterisks. Thus the appropriate interpretations are

1. The mean of the RHYME group is significantly lower than the means of the IMAGERY and ORGANIZA groups.
2. There is no significant difference between the means of the latter two groups.

GENERAL CHARACTERISTICS AND LIMITATIONS OF THE ONEWAY PROCEDURE

1. The number of cases or subjects in each group need not be equal.

FIGURE 9.9 Partial Output of Additional Analyses on Processing Strategies Experiment

```
- - - - - - - - - - - - - - - - - - - - - - - - - - - - - - O N E W A Y - - - - - - - - - - - - - - - - - - -

        VARIABLE   RECALL      NUMBER OF WORDS CORRECTLY RECALLED
     BY VARIABLE   STRATEGY    PROCESSING STRATEGIES

                               ANALYSIS OF VARIANCE

                                     SUM OF        MEAN          F        F
            SOURCE            D.F.    SQUARES       SQUARES     RATIO    PROB.

   BETWEEN GROUPS              2      730.7373     365.3686   34.1432   .0000

   WITHIN GROUPS              31      331.7333      10.7011

   TOTAL                      33     1062.4706


                                          STANDARD    STANDARD
   GROUP        COUNT     MEAN            DEVIATION     ERROR      MINIMUM     MAXIMUM    95 PCT CONF INT FOR MEAN

   IMAGERY       12      20.8333          3.6639      1.0577     15.0000     28.0000    18.5054 TO    23.1613
   ORGANIZA      12      22.1667          2.9181       .8424     17.0000     27.0000    20.3126 TO    24.0207
   RHYME         10      11.4000          3.1693      1.0022      7.0000     17.0000     9.1328 TO    13.6672

   TOTAL         34      18.5294          5.6742       .9731      7.0000     28.0000    16.5496 TO    20.5092



- - - - - - - - - - - - - - - - - - - - - - - - - - - - - - O N E W A Y - - - - - - - - - - - - - - - - - - -

        VARIABLE   RECALL      NUMBER OF WORDS CORRECTLY RECALLED
     BY VARIABLE   STRATEGY    PROCESSING STRATEGIES

   MULTIPLE RANGE TEST

   DUNCAN PROCEDURE
   RANGES FOR THE 0.050 LEVEL -

          2.88     3.03

   THE RANGES ABOVE ARE TABLE RANGES.
   THE VALUE ACTUALLY COMPARED WITH MEAN(J)-MEAN(I) IS..
          2.3131 * RANGE * DSQRT(1/N(I) + 1/N(J))

     (*) DENOTES PAIRS OF GROUPS SIGNIFICANTLY DIFFERENT AT THE 0.050 LEVEL

                                    R  I  O
                                    H  M  R
                                    Y  A  G
                                    M  G  A
                                    E  E  N
                                       R  I
                                       Y  Z
            MEAN        GROUP           Y  A

          11.4000      RHYME
          20.8333      IMAGERY         *
          22.1667      ORGANIZA        *  *
```

2. Only one independent variable can be included in a given ONEWAY command.

3. A maximum of 100 dependent variables may be specified on each ONEWAY procedure statement.

4. The independent variable can have as many levels, values, or groups as you wish. However, a posteriori comparisons with the subcommand RANGES cannot be performed on more than 50 group means.

5. No more than 10 RANGES subcommands can be requested with a ONEWAY command.

6. You should be aware of the possibility of exceeding the core storage space of your computer system. In this event, you can reduce your core storage requirements by using several ONEWAY commands, thereby reducing the number of dependent variables on each ONEWAY command.

10

ANOVA: Analysis of Variance for Factorial Designs

PURPOSE

ANOVA is the SPSS^x procedure for performing the analysis of variance on data from factorial designs. The defining characteristic of a factorial design is that it contains *two or more independent variables*. To illustrate, suppose you are interested in testing the effects of motivation level (low, medium, and high) and task difficulty (easy, difficult) on performance. In this 3 by 2 factorial design, there are two independent variables: motivation level and task difficulty. Further, there are three levels or values of motivation and two levels or values of task difficulty. The design that results from combining the possible values of these two independent variables follows.

		MOTIVATION LEVEL		
		LOW	MEDIUM	HIGH
TASK DIFFICULTY	EASY			
	DIFFICULT			

It should also be noted that the SPSS^x procedure ANOVA can be legitimately used only to analyze designs in which *all* of the independent variables are manipulated *between subjects*. That is, different subjects must be randomly assigned to each of the cells in the design. For example, the ANOVA procedure would be appropriate if you randomly assigned a certain number of subjects (e.g., 10) to each of the six cells in the preceding example (using a total of 60 subjects). If your factorial design contains a mixture of between-subjects and within-subjects variables (mixed design) or if it contains all within-subjects variables (repeated measures design), then you should use the MANOVA procedure described in the *SPSS*^{x} *User's Guide*.

The statistic that is calculated by ANOVA is the *F*-ratio, and an *F*-ratio is computed for each of the main effects and interactions.

GENERAL FORMAT OF THE ANOVA COMMAND

The general format for the ANOVA procedure is shown as follows. The abbreviations DV and IV refer to dependent variable and independent variable, respectively.

$$\text{ANOVA DV BY IV}_1 \begin{pmatrix} \text{minimum} & \text{maximum} \\ \text{value} & \text{, value} \end{pmatrix} \text{IV}_2 \begin{pmatrix} \text{minimum} & \text{maximum} \\ \text{value} & \text{, value} \end{pmatrix}$$

As shown, the dependent variable is typed before the word **BY**, and the independent variables follow the word **BY**. Independent variables are separated by spaces. Also, the minimum and maximum values must be specified after each independent variable. These values should be separated by a comma and enclosed within parentheses. Minimum and maximum values refer to the lowest and highest values or levels of the independent variables. Using the example described earlier, the three levels of the motivation variable might be coded as MOTIVE (1,3), and the two levels of task difficulty could be coded as TASKDIF (1,2). If performance is coded as PERF, appropriate ANOVA formats for analyzing this experiment are

```
ANOVA  PERF BY MOTIVE (1,3) TASKDIF (1,2)
```

or

```
ANOVA  PERF BY TASKDIF (1,2) MOTIVE (1,3)
```

Notice that the independent variables do not have to be listed in any particular order.

SPECIFYING MORE THAN ONE DEPENDENT VARIABLE

Several formats can be used when there are two or more dependent measures. As an example, assume that the experimenter for the study described previously collected measures on three types of performance

(PERFX, PERFY, PERFZ). To perform an analysis of variance for each of the three dependent variables, any of the following formats is appropriate:

```
ANOVA  PERFX BY MOTIVE (1,3) TASKDIF (1,2)/
       PERFY BY MOTIVE (1,3) TASKDIF (1,2)/
       PERFZ BY MOTIVE (1,3) TASKDIF (1,2)
```
or
```
ANOVA  PERFX PERFY PERFZ BY MOTIVE (1,3) TASKDIF (1,2)
```
or
```
ANOVA  PERFX TO PERFZ BY MOTIVE (1,3) TASKDIF (1,2)
```

Note that in the first example, up to five separate lists of dependent and independent variables may be requested with a single ANOVA command. (Three are shown here.) Also notice that when you request two or more lists of analyses with one ANOVA command, the lists must be separated by slashes. As you can see in the second and third examples, you can also request several analyses by listing dependent variables (separated by spaces) before the word BY, or by using the keyword TO. Regardless of which of these latter two methods you choose, *a maximum of five dependent variables* can be listed or indicated before the word BY. As shown subsequently, you can combine these techniques to request even more analyses.

```
ANOVA  PERFX TO PERFZ BY MOTIVE (1,3) TASKDIF (1,2)/
       MEAS1 TO MEAS5 BY MOTIVE (1,3) TASKDIF (1,2)/
       PERFY BY SEX (1,2) AGE (1,4)
```

If, for some reason, you cannot specify all of the analyses you need within the restrictions outlined previously, then you can simply add ANOVA commands to your SPSS^x file. When using the Within-File Method of reading data, remember that the additional ANOVA commands must follow the END DATA line.

SPECIFYING MORE THAN TWO INDEPENDENT VARIABLES

For factorial designs that contain more than two independent variables, simply list all of the independent variables (and their minimum and maximum values) after the word BY. You may specify up to 10 independent variables after the word BY. In the motivation level and task difficulty experiment, assume that you also varied the type of task (verbal, motor) to create a design with three independent variables. This 3 by 2 by 2 factorial design is diagrammed as follows.

VERBAL TASK
MOTIVATION LEVEL

		LOW	MEDIUM	HIGH
TASK DIFFICULTY	EASY			
	DIFFICULT			

MOTOR TASK
MOTIVATION LEVEL

		LOW	MEDIUM	HIGH
TASK DIFFICULTY	EASY			
	DIFFICULT			

An appropriate ANOVA statement for this design is

```
ANOVA  PERF BY MOTIVE (1,3) TASKDIF (1,2) TASKTYPE (1,2)
```

There are shortcuts for listing independent variables that have the same minimum and maximum values. Spaces or the keyword TO can be used to indicate a series of independent variables that have identical minimum and maximum values. The minimum and maximum values are typed only once—after the last independent variable in the series. For example, if you have three independent variables (VARA, VARB, VARC) and each of them has two levels, any of the following formats is appropriate:

```
ANOVA  PERF BY VARA (1,2) VARB (1,2) VARC (1,2)
```

or

```
ANOVA  PERF BY VARA VARB VARC (1,2)
```

or

```
ANOVA  PERF BY VARA TO VARC (1,2)
```

COMMONLY USED OPTIONS

There are 11 OPTIONS available with the ANOVA procedure. You may use some or none of these in your SPSS^x file. One of the most commonly used OPTIONS is described here, and the others are described in the ANOVA chapter of the *SPSS^x User's Guide.* Remember, if you decide to include an OPTIONS statement, it should appear on the line immediately following the ANOVA command.

OPTIONS 1

> Causes the scores of *all* subjects to be included in the analysis— even those that have been coded as missing data. If this option is used, all previous MISSING VALUES designations are ignored.

> If this option is not used, then the default option is invoked. That is, a case having a missing score or scores will be excluded from all of the analyses specified in your ANOVA command. For example, assume that a subject has missing data on dependent variable *A* but not on dependent variables *B* and *C*. If you listed dependent variables *A*, *B*, and *C* on a single ANOVA statement, then that subject will be omitted from *all three* analyses. If, however, you put dependent variable *A* on one ANOVA statement and dependent variables *B* and *C* on a different ANOVA statement, then that subject or case will be omitted from the analysis involving dependent variable *A* but not from the analyses involving dependent variables *B* and *C*.

COMMONLY USED STATISTICS

Three STATISTICS are available with ANOVA, and you may use none, some, or all of them. We have found one of these to be especially helpful, and it will be described subsequently. The other STATISTICS are used in conjunction with the analysis of covariance, and they can be found in the ANOVA chapter of the *SPSS^x User's Guide*. The STATISTICS command should be written on the line immediately following the OPTIONS command. If you do not include an OPTIONS statement, then the STATISTICS command should follow the ANOVA command.

STATISTICS 3

> Causes the means for all of the cells in the design and for all of the treatment conditions to appear on the printout.
> Additionally, the number of subjects that were included in the analysis from each group will be printed in the output.

The STATISTICS command should be omitted if no statistics are desired.

PUTTING THE SPSS^x FILE TOGETHER

Suppose that you conducted an experiment to test the effects of two independent variables (type of drug, dosage level) on aggression (dependent variable). Subjects in the experiment were given either small or large doses of either cocaine or alcohol. Then, their aggression was measured by the shock intensity they were willing to deliver to a confederate of the experiment. Thus, as shown, the design of this experiment was a 2 by 2 factorial.

	DOSAGE	
	SMALL	LARGE

DRUG COCAINE / ALCOHOL

The data sheet from this experiment appears in Figure 10.1, and you should try to write an SPSS^x program that performs the analysis of variance on these data. When you have written the SPSS^x file, check it with the one in Figure 10.2.

FIGURE 10.1 Data Sheet for Drug and Dosage Experiment

SUBJECT	DRUG CONDITION[a]	DOSAGE CONDITION[b]	AGGRESSION SCORE
01	1	1	6
02	1	1	3
.	.	.	.
.	.	.	.
.	.	.	.
10	1	1	5
11	1	2	2
12	1	2	7
.	.	.	.
.	.	.	.
.	.	.	.
20	1	2	4
21	2	1	5
22	2	1	4
.	.	.	.
.	.	.	.
.	.	.	.
30	2	1	3
31	2	2	12
32	2	2	14
.	.	.	.
.	.	.	.
.	.	.	.
40	2	2	18

[a]Code for drug condition: cocaine = 1, alcohol = 2
[b]Code for dosage condition: small = 1, large = 2

FIGURE 10.2   SPSSˣ File for Drug and Dosage Experiment

```
JOB...
EXEC SPSSX...                    (JCL commands for your computer system)
TITLE    "THE EFFECTS OF DRUG AND DOSAGE LEVEL ON AGGRESSION"
DATA LIST    /DRUG 4 DOSAGE 6 AGGRESS 8-9
VARIABLE LABELS    DRUG "TYPE OF DRUG"
                   DOSAGE "LEVEL OF DRUG DOSAGE"
                   AGGRESS "AGGRESSION OF SUBJECTS"
VALUE LABELS    DRUG 1 "COCAINE" 2 "ALCOHOL"/
                DOSAGE 1 "SMALL" 2 "LARGE"
ANOVA    AGGRESS BY DRUG DOSAGE (1,2)
STATISTICS    3
BEGIN DATA
01 1 1  6
02 1 1  3
.
.
.
10 1 1  5
11 1 2  2
12 1 2  7
.
.
.
20 1 2  4
21 2 1  5
22 2 1  4
.
.
.
30 2 1  3
31 2 2 12
32 2 2 14
.
.
.
40 2 2 18
END DATA
FINISH
END OF JOB...                    (JCL command for your computer system)
```

Notes and Variations

```
DATA LIST    /DRUG 4 DOSAGE 6 AGGRESS 8-9
```

> Given the format of the data lines, the preceding DATA LIST
> command is accurate. There are, however, more efficient ways
> of typing in your data. For example, you could have eliminated
> the subject numbers and the blank spaces between the values of
> the variables. Thus, if the data lines were typed in the
> following format

```
(Columns 1 . . 4 )
         ↓     ↓
         1 1   6
         1 1   3
          .
          .
          .
         1 1   5
         1 2   2
         1 2   7
          .
          .
          .
         1 2   4
         2 1   5
         2 1   4
          .
          .
          .
         2 1   3
         2 2 1 2
         2 2 1 4
          .
          .
          .
         2 2 1 8
```

the DATA LIST statement should look like the following one:

DATA LIST   /DRUG 1 DOSAGE 2 AGGRESS 3–4

VARIABLE LABELS   DRUG "TYPE OF DRUG"

> This causes the fuller description of your variable (up to 40 columns) to be printed on your output. This is an optional command.

VALUE LABELS   DRUG 1 "COCAINE" 2 "ALCOHOL"

> This causes the labels for the levels of your independent variables (in this case, COCAINE and ALCOHOL) to appear on the printout. This is an optional statement.

ANOVA   AGGRESS BY DRUG DOSAGE (1,2)

> Although this command is accurate, alternative forms for writing this command are listed as follows:
>
> ANOVA   AGGRESS BY DOSAGE DRUG (1,2)
>
> or
>
> ANOVA   AGGRESS BY DRUG (1,2) DOSAGE (1,2)

STATISTICS 3

This causes the number of subjects and means for all conditions to appear in the printout. Although optional, this is usually needed for interpreting the results.

Note that the variables listed in the VARIABLE LABELS, VALUE LABELS, and ANOVA commands *must be spelled exactly* as they appear in the DATA LIST statement.

You should now go on and work through the following examples. In these examples, an experiment with two dependent measures is presented, the SAVE and GET commands are used, and the printouts and explanations of the printouts are presented.

EXAMPLE 1: CORTICAL DESTRUCTION EXPERIMENT

A researcher was interested in examining the importance of the cerebral cortex on the learning of mazes by rats. The experimenter systematically studied the effects of destroying different amounts of the cerebral cortex and of variations in the complexity of the maze on performance. Thus, the two independent variables were

1. Percentage of cortex destroyed (0 percent, 25 percent, 50 percent)
2. Complexity of the maze (simple, complex)

The 3 by 2 factorial design that results from combining all possible levels of these two independent variables follows:

		PERCENT DESTRUCTION		
		0	25	50
MAZE COMPLEXITY	SIMPLE			
	COMPLEX			

Eight rats were randomly assigned to each of the six conditions in the design (using a total of 48 rats). Two dependent variables were measured: the total number of errors made and the total trials required to reach the learning criterion of running through the maze without error.

For this example, we want to perform two analyses of variance, one for each of the two dependent variables. The data sheet for this experiment is shown in Figure 10.3, and an appropriate SPSS[x] file for analyzing the data with the ANOVA procedure is presented in Figure 10.4.

Partial Output from the ANOVA Procedure

As mentioned previously, the SPSS[x] file in Figure 10.4 causes two analyses of variance to be computed, one for each of the two dependent

FIGURE 10.3 **Data Sheet for Cortical Destruction Experiment**

SUBJECT	CORTICAL DESTRUCTION[a]	MAZE COMPLEXITY[b]	ERRORS	TRIALS
01	1	1	17	8
02	1	1	24	15
.	.	.	.	.
.	.	.	.	.
.	.	.	.	.
08	1	1	20	12
09	1	2	70	21
10	1	2	72	21
.	.	.	.	.
.	.	.	.	.
.	.	.	.	.
16	1	2	67	15
17	2	1	26	15
18	2	1	31	10
.	.	.	.	.
.	.	.	.	.
.	.	.	.	.
24	2	1	34	19
25	2	2	305	43
26	2	2	290	38
.	.	.	.	.
.	.	.	.	.
.	.	.	.	.
32	2	2	318	40
33	3	1	40	15
34	3	1	48	18
.	.	.	.	.
.	.	.	.	.
.	.	.	.	.
40	3	1	53	23
41	3	2	820	88
42	3	2	785	85
.	.	.	.	.
.	.	.	.	.
.	.	.	.	.
48	3	2	1003	77

[a]Code for cortical destruction: 0 percent = 1, 25 percent = 2, 50 percent = 3
[b]Codes for maze complexity: simple = 1, complex = 2

FIGURE 10.4 **SPSS**[x] **File for Cortical Destruction Experiment**

```
JOB...
EXEC SPSSX...                (JCL commands for your computer system)
TITLE    "ANALYSES OF VARIANCE FOR CORTICAL DESTRUCTION EXPERIMENT"
FILE HANDLE  RATS01/local system specifications
DATA LIST    /CORTEX 4 MAZE 6 ERRORS 8-11 TRIALS 13-14
VARIABLE LABELS   CORTEX "PERCENT CORTICAL DESTRUCTION"
                  MAZE "COMPLEXITY OF MAZE"
                  ERRORS "NUMBER OF ERRORS TO CRITERION"
                  TRIALS "NUMBER OF TRIALS TO CRITERION"
VALUE LABELS    CORTEX 1 "0 PERCENT" 2 "25 PERCENT" 3 "50 PERCENT"/
                MAZE 1 "SIMPLE" 2 "COMPLEX"
ANOVA    ERRORS TRIALS BY CORTEX (1,3) MAZE (1,2)
STATISTICS    3
BEGIN DATA
01 1 1   17  8
02 1 1   24 15
 .
 .
 .
08 1 1   20 12
09 1 2   70 21
10 1 2   72 21
 .
 .
 .
16 1 2   67 15
17 2 1   26 15
18 2 1   31 10
 .
 .
 .
24 2 1   34 19
25 2 2  305 43
26 2 2  290 38
 .
 .
 .
32 2 2  318 40
33 3 1   40 15
34 3 1   48 18
 .
 .
 .
40 3 1   53 23
41 3 2  820 88
42 3 2  785 85
 .
 .
 .
48 3 2 1003 77
END DATA
SAVE  OUTFILE=RATS01
FINISH
END OF JOB...              (JCL command for your computer system)
```

---

variables (ERRORS, TRIALS). The output from the analysis performed on the TRIALS measure is listed in Figure 10.5. Because STATISTICS 3 was specified, the means for all conditions appear in the output. Also, the number of subjects or cases that make up each mean is printed in parentheses. To ensure that you understand these tables, each one is described subsequently.

FIGURE 10.5   Partial Output of the Analysis of Variance for the Cortical Destruction Experiment

```
ANALYSES OF VARIANCE FOR CORTICAL DESTRUCTION EXPERIMENT


                         * * * C E L L   M E A N S * * *
                 TRIALS      NUMBER O TRIALS TO CRITERION
              BY CORTEX      PERCENT CORTICAL DESTRUCTION
                 MAZE        COMPLEXITY OF MAZE


TOTAL POPULATION

     31.08
   (   48)


CORTEX
       1          2          3

     16.50      26.13      50.63
   (   16)  (     16)  (    16)


MAZE
       1          2

     15.58      46.58
   (   24)  (     24)


            MAZE
              1          2
CORTEX
     1      11.75      21.25
          (     8)  (     8)

     2      15.38      36.88
          (     8)  (     8)

     3      19.63      81.63
          (     8)  (     8)


           * * * A N A L Y S I S   O F   V A R I A N C E * * *
                 TRIALS      NUMBER O TRIALS TO CRITERION
              BY CORTEX      PERCENT CORTICAL DESTRUCTION
                 MAZE        COMPLEXITY OF MAZE

                             SUM OF                MEAN           SIGNIF
SOURCE OF VARIATION          SQUARES    DF        SQUARE     F     OF F

MAIN EFFECTS                21438.167    3       7146.056  269.058  0.000
    CORTEX                   9906.167    2       4953.083  186.490  0.0
    MAZE                    11532.000    1      11532.000  434.195  0.000

2-WAY INTERACTIONS           6054.000    2       3027.000  113.970  0.0
    CORTEX   MAZE            6054.000    2       3027.000  113.970  0.0

EXPLAINED                   27492.167    5       5498.433  207.023  0.000

RESIDUAL                     1115.500   42         26.560

TOTAL                       28607.667   47        608.674


     48 CASES WERE PROCESSED.
      0 CASES (  0.0 PCT) WERE MISSING.
```

TOTAL POPULATION

    31.08 Grand mean
(48) Number of cases

> This number is the grand mean that represents the mean number of trials to reach criterion for all 48 subjects.

CORTEX

1	2	3
16.50	26.13	50.63
(16)	(16)	(16)

> These means are used to interpret a possible main effect of the cortical destruction variable. They are computed by ignoring the maze complexity variable and calculating the average trials to criterion for the 16 subjects in each of the three cortical destruction conditions. Levels 1, 2, and 3 stand for 0 percent, 25 percent, and 50 percent cortical destruction, respectively.

MAZE

1	2
15.58	46.58
(24)	(24)

> These means are used to evaluate a possible main effect of the maze complexity variable. They represent the mean trials to criterion for the subjects in the simple and complex maze conditions (24 subjects in each condition). The numbers 1 and 2 represent the simple and complex mazes, respectively.

	MAZE	
	1	2
CORTEX		
1	11.75	21.25
	(8)	(8)
2	15.38	36.88
	(8)	(8)
3	19.63	81.63
	(8)	(8)

> These are the means for each of the six cells in the design. They are important for evaluating the interaction between the two independent variables.

The analysis of variance table is printed after the means. As shown, the source of variation, sum of squares, degrees of freedom, mean square, F-ratio and probability level of the F-ratio are listed for each main effect and interaction. This table also includes the sum of squares, degrees of freedom, and mean square of the RESIDUAL (denominator or error term of the F-ratio). You will notice that in all of these cases SIGNIF OF F is printed as .000. This means that the probability level of the F-ratio is *less than* .001. Thus, in this particular example, both main effects (CORTEX,

MAZE) and the interaction (CORTEX by MAZE) are significant (at the .001 alpha level).

EXAMPLE 2: CORTICAL DESTRUCTION EXPERIMENT— ADDITIONAL ANALYSIS

Suppose now that the experimenter wanted to examine the effects of the two independent variables on the average number of errors made on each trial (RATE). This measure can be derived by dividing the total number of errors to reach criterion by the total number of trials to reach criterion for each subject (using the COMPUTE command). Because the data from the previous analysis were saved in file RATS01, the GET command can be used to perform the additional analysis. An appropriate SPSS^x file is presented in Figure 10.6, and the output is shown in Figure 10.7.

GENERAL CHARACTERISTICS AND LIMITATIONS OF THE ANOVA PROCEDURE

1. The number of cases or subjects in each group does not have to be equal.
2. All of the independent variables must be manipulated between subjects.
3. The ANOVA procedure *cannot* be used for analyzing designs that contain more than 10 independent variables.
4. No more than five dependent variables can be specified before the word BY, and no more than five dependent and independent variable lists can be specified in a single ANOVA command. If you have more than five dependent variables or more than five lists, use additional ANOVA procedure statements after the END DATA statement.
5. The ANOVA procedure does not compute a posteriori comparisons (described in Chapter 9). If you have a factorial design and you need to perform

FIGURE 10.6   SPSS^x File for Additional Analysis on Cortical Destruction Experiment

```
JOB. . .
EXEC SPSSX. . .                 (JCL commands for your computer system)
TITLE  "ANOVA FOR ADDITIONAL ANALYSIS"
FILE HANDLE  RATS01/local system specifications
GET  FILE=RATS01
COMPUTE  RATE=ERRORS/TRIALS
VARIABLE LABELS  RATE "ERRORS PER TRIAL"
ANOVA  RATE BY CORTEX (1,3) MAZE (1,2)
STATISTICS  3
FINISH
END OF JOB. . .                 (JCL command for your computer system)
```

a posteriori comparisons, you can find formulas for performing these comparisons in most advanced statistics texts.

6. Although it is very unlikely, you may go beyond the core storage space available on your computer system. If this should happen, you can decrease your demand for storage space by using several ANOVA commands and/or by reducing the number of dependent variables that you specify on each procedure statement. (Consult the *SPSS^x User's Guide* for other limitations.)

FIGURE 10.7   Output of Additional Analysis on the Cortical Destruction Experiment

```
ANOVA FOR ADDITIONAL ANALYSIS


                        * * * C E L L   M E A N S * * *
                    RATE        ERRORS PER TRIAL
                 BY CORTEX      PERCENT CORTICAL DESTRUCTION
                    MAZE        COMPLEXITY OF MAZE


TOTAL POPULATION

        4.66
   (     48)


CORTEX
        1            2            3

      2.54         4.86         6.58
   (    16)  (      16)  (      16)


MAZE
        1            2

      2.00         7.32
   (    24)  (      24)


             MAZE
               1            2
CORTEX
      1        1.59         3.49
           (     8)  (       8)

      2        1.98         7.73
           (     8)  (       8)

      3        2.41        10.75
           (     8)  (       8)



           * * * A N A L Y S I S   O F   V A R I A N C E * * *
                    RATE        ERRORS PER TRIAL
                 BY CORTEX      PERCENT CORTICAL DESTRUCTION
                    MAZE        COMPLEXITY OF MAZE
```

SOURCE OF VARIATION	SUM OF SQUARES	DF	MEAN SQUARE	F	SIGNIF OF F
MAIN EFFECTS	472.020	3	157.340	261.077	0.000
CORTEX	131.334	2	65.667	108.962	0.0
MAZE	340.686	1	340.686	565.306	0.000
2-WAY INTERACTIONS	84.100	2	42.050	69.774	0.0
CORTEX MAZE	84.100	2	42.050	69.774	0.0
EXPLAINED	556.120	5	111.224	184.556	0.000
RESIDUAL	25.312	42	0.603		
TOTAL	581.431	47	12.371		

```
        48 CASES WERE PROCESSED.
         0 CASES (  0.0 PCT) WERE MISSING.
```

11

PEARSON CORR and SCATTERGRAM: Pearson Product-Moment Correlation and Scattergram Plotting of Results

PURPOSE

The PEARSON CORR procedure is used to obtain Pearson product-moment correlation coefficients (r's) for pairs of variables and to test the significance of these coefficients. Thus you can find the direction and degree of relationship between any two continuous variables obtained in your study. You may also want to graph the relationships between your variables (i.e., create scatterplots). This can be accomplished with the procedure SCATTERGRAM, which is also described in this chapter.

GENERAL FORMAT OF THE PEARSON CORR COMMAND

```
PEARSON CORR  VAR1 VAR2 . . . WITH VARA VARB . . .
```

After the PEARSON CORR command, you list the variables that you wish to have correlated. The word WITH sets up the pairs of variables that are to be correlated (e.g., VAR1 with VARA, VAR1 with VARB, VAR2 with VARA, VAR2 with VARB). Another example follows.

```
PEARSON CORR  AGE INCOME WEIGHT WITH IQ BMR
```

Here you are requesting six correlation coefficients: AGE with IQ, AGE with BMR, INCOME with IQ, INCOME with BMR, WEIGHT with IQ, and WEIGHT with BMR.

VARIATIONS IN FORMAT

If you wish to compute all possible correlations among your listed variables (a complete correlation matrix), you can simply list all of the variables once and omit the word WITH.

```
PEARSON CORR  AGE SEX IQ
```

is the same as

```
PEARSON CORR  AGE SEX IQ WITH AGE SEX IQ
```

Even more conveniently, you can use the word TO to signify inclusion of all variables between the first and last specified.

```
PEARSON CORR  Q1 TO Q4
```

is the same as

```
PEARSON CORR  Q1 Q2 Q3 Q4
```

which is the same as

```
PEARSON CORR  Q1 Q2 Q3 Q4 WITH Q1 Q2 Q3 Q4
```

You may request several different sets of correlations or matrices with a single PEARSON CORR command—just use slashes to separate them.

```
PEARSON CORR  Q1 Q2 Q5 WITH Q7/Q3 WITH Q9 TO Q11/Q6 TO Q10
```

COMMONLY USED OPTIONS

There are six OPTIONS available with PEARSON CORR. You may specify some or none of these OPTIONS in your SPSS^x file. A brief description of the four OPTIONS commands that you are most likely to see follows. For the entire set, see the PEARSON CORR chapter in the *SPSS^x User's Guide*. The OPTIONS command, if used, follows the PEARSON CORR command.

```
OPTIONS  1
```

Causes all subjects to be included in all calculations even if there are missing data coded on that subject's record.

OPTIONS 2

> Causes a subject to be dropped from *all* analyses in a given PEARSON CORR statement if there are missing data for *any* of the variables listed on that PEARSON CORR statement.

> If you do not specify OPTIONS 1 or 2, a subject or case is eliminated from only the calculations involving the missing information. Thus, if there are three variables to be correlated (*A*, *B*, and *C*) and a case has missing data only on variable *B*, then that case will be excluded from the correlations of *A* with *B* and *B* with *C*, but not from the correlation of *A* with *C*.

OPTIONS 3

> Specifies a two-tailed test of significance instead of the default procedure of a one-tailed test. The one-tailed test is used when you have a predicted direction of correlation in mind.

OPTIONS 6

> Causes only the nonredundant coefficients to be printed when you have requested that all pairwise correlations be executed. That is, your printout would have the coefficient for VAR1 with VAR2 but would not repeat the redundant coefficient for VAR2 with VAR1.

To invoke more than one option, simply list the numbers, separated by spaces.

OPTIONS 1 3 6

The OPTIONS command may be omitted altogether if none of the possible options is desired.

COMMONLY USED STATISTICS

You may choose one, both, or neither of the two STATISTICS available with PEARSON CORR. (Both are described in the *SPSS^x User's Guide.*) One that is commonly used is

STATISTICS 1

> Causes the means and standard deviations of each variable in the PEARSON CORR statement to be calculated and printed.

The STATISTICS command, if used, follows the OPTIONS command. It may be omitted entirely.

PUTTING THE SPSSˣ FILE TOGETHER

To test your understanding of the SPSSˣ program for Pearson product-moment correlation, try to set up the SPSSˣ commands to test for a correlation between temperature and crime rate in the example that follows. Suppose that you have determined for a given city both the daily high temperature and the arrest rate for 24 days distributed over a 12-month period. Your data sheet might look like that in Figure 11.1. Try to write your SPSSˣ program and then check your file against the one in Figure 11.2.

Notes and Variations

```
DATA LIST   /TEMP 6-8 CRIME 10-12
```

You might note that the data were coded with a date for identification purposes. Thus the value of the first variable (TEMP) does not appear until column 6. Spaces were also included to enhance the visual display of the data on the computer screen. Neither identification nor spacing is necessary. We could have typed the data lines as follows:

```
Columns 1....6
        ↓    ↓
       -10 50
       -15 96
         6 62
         .
         .
         .
       10101
```

The DATA LIST command would be revised accordingly:

```
DATA LIST   /TEMP 1-3 CRIME 4-6
```

FIGURE 11.1   Data Sheet for Correlation of Temperature and Crime Rate

DATE	HIGH TEMPERATURE	ARRESTS
0113	−10 C	50
0125	−15 C	96
0203	6 C	62
.	.	.
.	.	.
1216	10 C	101

FIGURE 11.2   SPSSˣ File for the Correlation of Temperature and Crime Rate

```
JOB...
EXEC SPSSX...              (JCL commands for your computer system)
TITLE   "CORRELATION OF TEMPERATURE AND CRIME RATE"
DATA LIST    /TEMP 6-8 CRIME 10-12
VARIABLE LABELS    TEMP "CENTIGRADE TEMPERATURE HIGH"
                   CRIME "NUMBER OF CRIMINAL ARRESTS"
PEARSON CORR    TEMP WITH CRIME
BEGIN DATA
0113 -10  50
0125 -15  96
0203   6  62
.

.

.
1216  10 101
END DATA
FINISH
END OF JOB...          (JCL command for your computer system)
```

```
VARIABLE LABELS  TEMP "CENTIGRADE TEMPERATURE HIGH"
```

> This optional command provides fuller labels (up to 40 columns) for the variables on the printout for easier interpretation.

```
PEARSON CORR  TEMP WITH CRIME
```

> This command could also have been written:
>
> ```
> PEARSON CORR  TEMP CRIME
> ```
>
> No STATISTICS or OPTIONS were specified for this analysis; however, it is generally helpful to request descriptive statistics (STATISTICS 1).

Note that the variables listed in the **VARIABLE LABELS** and **PEARSON CORR** statements *must be spelled exactly* as they appear in the **DATA LIST** statement.

You are now ready to go on to further examples that will illustrate other aspects of the PEARSON CORR procedure. These examples will give you sample data sets, SPSSˣ files, printouts, and descriptions of the printouts. They also illustrate the use of some of the additional commands described in Chapter 3.

EXAMPLE 1: DORMITORY SURVEY

Suppose that you have collected questionnaire responses to five questions concerning satisfaction with dormitory conditions from 50 college freshmen. You have also assessed their family's annual income level and their SAT scores. You would like to test the hypotheses that satisfaction with the college living environment is correlated with wealth (family income) and academic aptitude (SAT scores).

The questionnaire contains four questions about satisfaction with various aspects of the dormitory room: size, location, color, furnishings. These are answered on 5-point Likert-type scales (very dissatisfied to very satisfied), which are coded as 1 to 5. The fifth question asks for an estimate of the number of hours per day that are spent in the room.

First, we will set up the simplest version of this analysis—with no missing data and no data modification. Your data sheet might look like that in Figure 11.3, and your SPSS[x] file should look like that in Figure 11.4.

In the correlation example presented here, we have requested all pairwise correlations among our seven variables. Thus we can see the hypothesized relationships between income and SAT and the individual questionnaire responses, plus the correlations among the questionnaire response themselves. We have also asked for only nonredundant coefficients (OPTIONS 6) and have requested means and standard deviations for all variables (STATISTICS 1). The printout that you will get for this analysis is presented in Figure 11.5. We have also used the FILE HANDLE and SAVE commands to create an SPSS[x] system file.

FIGURE 11.3   Data Sheet for Dormitory Survey

			QUESTIONNAIRE RESPONSES				
SUBJECT	INCOME[a]	SAT[b]	1	2	3	4	5
01	19	1260	4	5	5	4	12
02	30	840	3	3	5	5	19
03	45	1020	2	1	2	2	8
04	25	1500	5	3	4	4	10
05	70	1460	1	1	1	1	5
.	.	.	.	.	.	.	.
.	.	.	.	.	.	.	.
.	.	.	.	.	.	.	.
50	56	980	2	1	3	2	5

[a]To the nearest thousand
[b]Total of math and verbal scores

After the word SCATTERGRAM, leave at least one space and then type the list of variables for which plots are to be constructed. The first variable in the list will be plotted on the y-axis, and the second variable will be plotted on the x-axis. More than two variables can be listed as shown:

```
SCATTERGRAM  VAR1 VAR2 VAR3 VAR4
```

In this example, six plots would result: VAR1 with VAR2, VAR1 with VAR3, VAR1 with VAR4, VAR2 with VAR3, VAR2 with VAR4, and VAR3 with VAR4. These plots could also be requested with the following format:

```
SCATTERGRAM  VAR1 TO VAR4
```

If the word WITH is used, as in PEARSON CORR, you can designate specific pairings for plotting. For example

```
SCATTERGRAM  VAR1 VAR2 W1TH VAR3 VAR4
```

would result in the following pairings for scatterplots: VAR1 with VAR3, VAR1 with VAR4, VAR2 with VAR3, and VAR2 with VAR4.

Separate sets of variables can be included in the same SCATTERGRAM statement if separated by slashes (/). For example

```
SCATTERGRAM  VAR1 VAR2 VAR3/VAR10 TO VAR13
```

Remember that SCATTERGRAM is a procedure statement and must follow the general rules for placement in the file; that is, only one procedure statement can be included before the BEGIN DATA statement. Others must go after the END DATA statement. Thus, in Figure 11.4 the SCATTERGRAM statement should follow the END DATA statement. In Figure 11.6, the SCATTERGRAM statement should precede the FINISH statement.

For further information about SCATTERGRAM, consult that chapter in the *SPSS^x User's Guide*. An example of output for this procedure is given in Figure 11.8 for the variable pair INCOME and Q1 (satisfaction with room size) from the dormitory study. On the graph, note that a single case is represented by an asterisk (*). More than one case (up to eight cases) is represented by the actual number, and nine or more cases is indicated by a 9.

LIMITATIONS OF PEARSON CORR

1. You cannot request more than 40 different sets of correlations or matrices with a single PEARSON CORR command.
2. You cannot have more than 250 individual elements with a single PEARSON CORR command. This includes every time you use a variable name (and its

FIGURE 11.8 Scattergram for the Variables of Income and Satisfaction with Room Size from the Dormitory Study

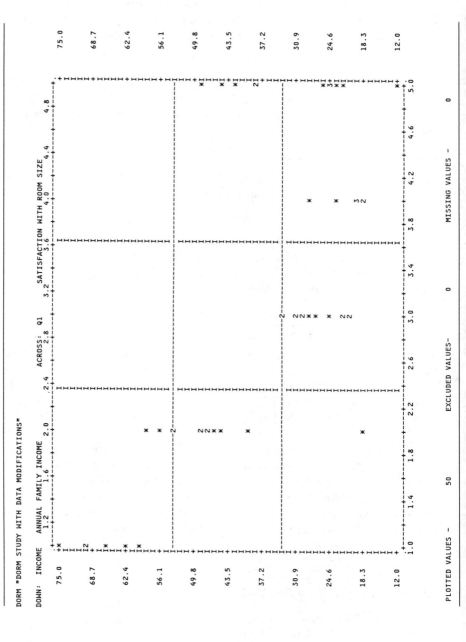

repetitions), words like TO and WITH, and any other special terms. It does not include variables implied by the keyword TO.

3. Regardless of the number of individual elements, you cannot have more than 500 variables named or implied with a single PEARSON CORR command. This includes repetitions in different sets of correlations requested.

4. You cannot exceed the core storage space of your computer system; you may therefore have to reduce your requests to adjust to the available storage.

It is unlikely that you will exceed these four limitations while you are learning SPSS[x], but do remember that they exist. A problem can usually be solved by breaking your requests down into shorter sets. You may use the GET procedure for other requests, or you can include additional PEARSON CORR commands after the END DATA line.

12

REGRESSION: Multiple Regression Analysis

The REGRESSION procedure is used to perform multiple regression analyses. It allows the researcher to examine the degree of relationship between a particular dependent variable and one or more independent variables. With this procedure, different linear equations (i.e., different sets and orderings of the independent variables) are compared to find the best model for the prediction of the dependent variable. Also, both the combined and relative predictive ability of the independent variables can be determined. Although multiple regression is an extension of correlation (covered in Chapter 11), it is not a simple one, and we strongly urge you to consult appropriate resources for guidance in the use and interpretation of this statistic.

To illustrate the use of multiple regression analysis, suppose that you wished to develop a prediction equation for college freshman grade point averages (FGPAs). You have decided to test for the relative contributions of the following independent variables (predictors): scholastic aptitude test score (SAT), high school grade point average (HSGPA), and socioeconomic status of family (SES). Data would be obtained on a sample of students for whom all four pieces of information are available: SAT, HSGPA, SES, and

FGPA. (If a successful prediction model is generated, then it could be used to predict the FGPA for future students from the same population.) By comparing different numbers, combinations, and orderings of the independent variables for covariation with the dependent variable, the multiple regression analysis will yield the best prediction equation. It will give the total contribution of the set of predictors (multiple correlation coefficient—R) and the relative contribution of each predictor (B and BETA weights). Tests of statistical significance will be provided for the overall model and for each predictor.

GENERAL FORMAT OF THE REGRESSION COMMAND

The REGRESSION procedure makes use of certain keywords to carry out the various options and statistics available within the program. (In most other procedures, these variations have been specified in separate OPTIONS and STATISTICS commands.) In presenting the general format here, we will deal with only the most commonly used specifications and, after giving you an overview, explain each in detail. The general format for the procedure is

```
REGRESSION  DESCRIPTIVES/
            VARIABLES=list of all of the variables to be included
                      in the equations/
            DEPENDENT=name of dependent variable/
            STEPWISE (or other method of evaluating equations)/
```

1. DESCRIPTIVES/

This is an *optional* subcommand used to request basic descriptive statistics to be printed for the variables: means, standard deviations, correlations. If this command is not included, no descriptive statistics will be printed. For descriptive statistics other than mean, standard deviation, and correlation, consult the REGRESSION chapter in the *SPSS^x User's Guide*.

2. VARIABLES= . . . /

This is a *necessary* subcommand used to indicate which variables from the DATA LIST command are being considered in the regression analysis. All of the dependent and independent variables must be included in this statement. Variable names are separated with a space, and the entire set is followed by a slash (/).

```
VARIABLES=VARA VARB VARC VARD/
```

An inclusive series of variables may be indicated with the word TO. Thus another way to write the preceding example is

```
VARIABLES=VARA TO VARD/
```

3. DEPENDENT= . . . /

> This is a *necessary* subcommand used to indicate which variable from the VARIABLES= list is specified as the dependent variable. For example
>
> DEPENDENT=VARD/
>
> Although a given prediction equation has only one dependent variable, you may specify more than one dependent variable in this command. Separate regression analyses will be computed for each dependent variable listed (and will exclude the other dependent variables listed from consideration as independent variables). For example
>
> VARIABLES=VARA TO VARD/
> DEPENDENT=VARD VARC/
>
> Such a specification would cause two regression analyses to be performed—one with VARD as the dependent variable and VARA and VARB as independent variables and one with VARC as the dependent variable and VARA and VARB as the independent variables. Neither dependent variable is used as an independent variable in either equation. (Other formats, to be described subsequently, may be used to have a dependent variable in one equation included as an independent variable in another equation.)

4. STEPWISE/

> This is one of six available statistical methods for evaluating possible prediction equations to reach the best model. The other five are FORWARD, BACKWARD, ENTER, REMOVE and TEST. Here we will describe only the STEPWISE method. You may consult the REGRESSION chapter in the *SPSS^x User's Guide* for brief descriptions of the other methods.
>
> STEPWISE requests the *stepwise regression procedure* to be used in equation construction and comparison. In this procedure, the first equation constructed has only one independent variable—the one most highly correlated with the dependent variable. If the *F*-test value for that regression equation is significant, a second independent variable is entered—the one with the next highest significant partial correlation with the dependent variable (after the variability accounted for by the first variable has been partialed out or removed). This procedure is continued until all independent variables with significant partial correlations have been included. Each subsequent equation is checked for changes in the significance of previous independent variables, resulting from the addition of other predictors. That is, the first variable to be included may have been the best single predictor but of significantly less predictive value once others, with which it overlaps, are added. Thus, once in the equation, variables do not necessarily remain in the equation as progressive entries and comparisons are made. You end up, then, with the *best set* of statistically significant predictors of the dependent variable.

REQUESTING SEVERAL REGRESSION ANALYSES

With a single REGRESSION command, you can request more than one analysis. There are three ways of doing this.

1. Use more than one VARIABLES= set of subcommands.

```
REGRESSION  DESCRIPTIVES/
            VARIABLES=VARA TO VARD/
            DEPENDENT=VARA/
            STEPWISE/
            DESCRIPTIVES/
            VARIABLES=VARE TO VARH/
            DEPENDENT=VARH/
            STEPWISE
```

This would allow you to examine two totally different sets of variables from the DATA LIST command. Notice that a new DESCRIPTIVES statement is needed for the second VARIABLES= list. From this set of subcommands, you would obtain one stepwise regression analysis with VARA as the dependent variable and VARB, VARC, and VARD entered as possible independent variables and another stepwise regression analysis with VARH as the dependent variable and VARE, VARF, and VARG entered as possible independent variables.

You may type the lines differently as long as you indent at least one space to show continuation of the REGRESSION command to new lines and as long as you keep the slashes located properly to separate the subcommands. No slash is needed for the last subcommand listed. For example, your REGRESSION command might look like this:

```
REGRESSION  DESCRIPTIVES/VARIABLES=VARA TO
            VARD/DEPENDENT=VARA/STEPWISE/
            DESCRIPTIVES/VARIABLES=VARE TO
            VARH/DEPENDENT=VARH/STEPWISE
```

2. Use more than one variable name in the DEPENDENT= statement (as described earlier).

```
REGRESSION  DESCRIPTIVES/
            VARIABLES=VARA TO VARD/
            DEPENDENT=VARA VARB/
            STEPWISE
```

Here, the same variable set is being examined but with two different dependent variables. Neither dependent variable specified will be included as a predictor in the equation for the other. Thus the first regression analysis will have VARA as the dependent variable, with VARC and VARD entered as possible independent variables. The second regression analysis will have VARB as the dependent variable, with VARC and VARD entered as possible independent variables.

3. Use more than one DEPENDENT= statement.

```
REGRESSION  DESCRIPTIVES/
            VARIABLES=VARA TO VARD/
```

```
DEPENDENT=VARA/
STEPWISE/
DEPENDENT=VARB/
STEPWISE
```

In contrast with method 2, this specification allows each dependent variable to be retained as a predictor in all equations other than the one in which it is the specified criterion (dependent variable). Thus, in this example, two regression analyses will be computed. In the first analysis, VARA will be the dependent variable and VARB, VARC, and VARD will be entered as possible independent variables. In the second analysis, VARB will be the dependent variable and VARA, VARC, and VARD will be entered as possible independent variables.

MISSING DATA

If some cases have incomplete data, you need to consider the alternative ways of dealing with these missing values. If no specification is made, the computer will delete the entire record of the subject if there is missing information on any of the variables in the VARIABLES= statement. If there are frequent instances of missing data, this is the best option for accurate statistical inference; however, it may lower the sample size to an undesirable number.

Alternately, you may include a subcommand MISSING=PAIRWISE/ to request that a subject's record be dropped only from calculations involving the missing information and not from calculations for which the subject has valid scores.

The command MISSING=MEANSUBSTITUTION/ replaces missing values with the variable mean, thereby using all cases.

The command MISSING=INCLUDE/ results in the inclusion of all cases in all analyses, even those with values coded as missing.

If you include a MISSING= command, it should appear immediately before the VARIABLES= statement as shown:

```
REGRESSION  DESCRIPTIVES/
            MISSING=PAIRWISE/
            VARIABLES=VARA TO VARD/
            DEPENDENT=VARD/
            STEPWISE
```

PUTTING THE SPSS^X FILE TOGETHER

To try out your understanding of this procedure, write an SPSS^X program for the following example. Imagine that you wanted to see if job absenteeism in a large factory can be predicted from two variables: employee age and employee education level. For each of 50 randomly selected employees, you have the number of absences during a one-year period and the employee's age and number of years of formal education. Use the data shown in Figure 12.1 to write an SPSS^x program that performs the regression analysis for these variables. Then, compare your SPSS^x program with the one in Figure 12.2.

Notes and Variations

```
DATA LIST  /ABSENCES 4-5 AGE 6-7 ED 8-9
```

> This command is appropriate for the way these data are typed in. Remember that you may use alternative ways of entering data, for example, omitting identification numbers and spaces. Thus another way of entering the data of this example could be

```
(Columns 1....6)
        ↓   ↓
       23614
       132512
        652 9
          .
          .
          .
       151913
```

> The DATA LIST command would be changed accordingly:

```
DATA LIST  /ABSENCES 1-2 AGE 3-4 ED 5-6
```

```
VARIABLE LABELS  ABSENCES "NUMBER OF ABSENCES"
```

> The VARIABLE LABELS statement is optional but often serves to clarify the printout. You do not have to provide labels for all variables. We could have provided labels for ABSENCES and ED, and not for AGE.

Note that the variables listed in the VARIABLE LABELS and REGRESSION statements *must be spelled exactly* as they appear in the DATA LIST statement.

FIGURE 12.1 Data Sheet for Regression Analysis on Job Absenteeism

SUBJECT	ABSENCES	AGE	EDUCATION
01	2	36	14
02	13	25	12
03	6	52	9
.	.	.	.
.	.	.	.
.	.	.	.
50	15	19	13

FIGURE 12.2   SPSSˣ File for Regression Analysis on Job Absenteeism

```
JOB...
EXEC SPSSX...                    (JCL commands for your computer system)
TITLE    "REGRESSION ANALYSIS TO PREDICT ABSENTEEISM"
DATA LIST    /ABSENCES 4-5 AGE 6-7 ED 8-9
VARIABLE LABELS    ABSENCES "NUMBER OF ABSENCES"
                   AGE "EMPLOYEE AGE"
                   ED "EMPLOYEE YEARS OF FORMAL SCHOOLING"
REGRESSION    DESCRIPTIVES/
              VARIABLES=ABSENCES AGE ED/
              DEPENDENT=ABSENCES/
              STEPWISE
BEGIN DATA
01  23614
02 132512
03  652 9
 .

 .

 .
50 151913
END DATA
FINISH
END OF JOB...            (JCL command for your computer system)
```

EXAMPLE 1: PREDICTING FRESHMAN GRADE POINT AVERAGES

Suppose you wish to determine the best set of predictors to account for the variations in college FGPAs. You have been able to obtain the following information for your current sample: freshman grade point averages (FGPA), sex (SEX), type of high school—public or private—(HSTYPE), a 10-point index of extracurricular activities in high school (EXTRA), a 7-point index of parents' socioeconomic status (SES), Scholastic Aptitude Test scores (SAT), and high school grade point averages (HSGPA). Your data sheet might look like the one shown in Figure 12.3, and your SPSSˣ file like Figure 12.4. Figure 12.5 shows the output.

Output from REGRESSION Procedure

The first section of the printout contains the means, standard deviations, and correlation matrix of the variables as requested in the DESCRIPTIVES/ command. The remainder of the printout shows each step in the stepwise regression analysis beginning with the variable correlated most highly with the dependent variable.

At each step (each new variable entry), you are first given an overall analysis (multiple R, R^2, and analysis of variance on the existing model).

FIGURE 12.3 Data Sheet for Prediction of Freshman Grade Point Averages

SUBJECT	SEX[a]	HSTYPE[b]	EXTRA	SES	SAT[c]	HSGPA	FGPA
001	1	2	8	4	99	2.9	3.8
002	1	2	2	5	78	3.5	2.0
003	2	1	7	3	83	4.0	3.5
004	1	2	5	7	80	3.0	1.9
005	2	1	7	2	95	3.0	3.5
.	.	.	.	.	.	.	.
.	.	.	.	.	.	.	.
.	.	.	.	.	.	.	.
100	2	1	6	7	90	3.2	2.5

[a]Code for sex: male = 1, female = 2
[b]Code for high school type: private = 1, public = 2
[c]Presented as percentile ranks

FIGURE 12.4 SPSS[x] File for Prediction of Freshman Grade Point Averages

```
JOB...
EXEC SPSSX...              (JCL commands for your computer system)
TITLE      "REGRESSION ANALYSIS TO PREDICT FRESHMAN GRADES"
FILE HANDLE    FGPA1/local system specifications
DATA LIST   /SEX 5 HSTYPE 7 EXTRA 9 SES 11 SAT 13-14 HSGPA 16-18 FGPA 20-22
VARIABLE LABELS    HSTYPE "HIGH SCHOOL TYPE"
                   EXTRA "EXTRACURRICULAR ACTIVITIES"
                   SES "SOCIOECONOMIC CLASS"
                   SAT "SCHOLASTIC APTITUDE TEST PERFORMANCE"
                   HSGPA "HIGH SCHOOL GRADE POINT AVERAGE"
                   FGPA "FRESHMAN GRADE POINT AVERAGE"
VALUE LABELS    SEX 1 "MALE" 2 "FEMALE"/
                HSTYPE 1 "PRIVATE" 2 "PUBLIC"
REGRESSION    DESCRIPTIVES/
              VARIABLES=EXTRA TO FGPA/
              DEPENDENT=FGPA/
              STEPWISE
BEGIN DATA
001 1 2 8 4 99 2.9 3.8
002 1 2 2 5 78 3.5 2.0
003 2 1 7 3 83 4.0 3.5
004 1 2 5 7 80 3.0 1.9
005 2 1 7 2 95 3.0 3.5
.
.

100 2 1 6 7 90 3.2 2.5
END DATA
SAVE    OUTFILE=FGPA1
FINISH
END OF JOB...              (JCL command for your computer system)
```

FIGURE 12.5 Output of Regression Analysis on Freshman Grade Point Average Data

REGRESSION ANALYSIS TO PREDICT FRESHMAN GRADES

```
                    * * * *   M U L T I P L E   R E G R E S S I O N   * * * *
```

VARIABLE LIST NUMBER 1   LISTWISE DELETION OF MISSING DATA

	MEAN	STD DEV	LABEL
EXTRA	4.780	1.840	EXTRACURRICULAR ACTIVITIES
SES	3.720	1.886	SOCIOECONOMIC CLASS
SAT	79.160	11.792	SCHOLASTIC APTITUDE TEST PERFORMANCE
HSGPA	2.708	.596	HIGH SCHOOL GRADE POINT AVERAGE
FGPA	2.930	.611	FRESHMAN GRADE POINT AVERAGE

N OF CASES =   100

CORRELATION:

	EXTRA	SES	SAT	HSGPA	FGPA
EXTRA	1.000	-.420	.337	-.003	.316
SES	-.420	1.000	-.353	-.059	-.278
SAT	.337	-.353	1.000	.367	.656
HSGPA	-.003	-.059	.367	1.000	.529
FGPA	.316	-.278	.656	.529	1.000

```
                    * * * *   M U L T I P L E   R E G R E S S I O N   * * * *
```

VARIABLE LIST NUMBER 1   LISTWISE DELETION OF MISSING DATA
EQUATION NUMBER 1   DEPENDENT VARIABLE..   FGPA   FRESHMAN GRADE POINT AVERAGE
  DESCRIPTIVE STATISTICS ARE PRINTED ON PAGE   3
BEGINNING bLOCK NUMBER   1.   METHOD: STEPWISE

VARIABLE(S) ENTERED ON STEP NUMBER   1..   SAT   SCHOLASTIC APTITUDE TEST PERFORMANCE

MULTIPLE R	.65560		ANALYSIS OF VARIANCE	DF	SUM OF SQUARES	MEAN SQUARE
R SQUARE	.42982		REGRESSION	1	15.89891	15.89891
ADJUSTED R SQUARE	.42400		RESIDUAL	98	21.09109	.21522
STANDARD ERROR	.46391					

F =   73.87451   SIGNIF F =   .0000

```
------------ VARIABLES IN THE EQUATION ------------
```

VARIABLE	B	SE B	BETA	T	SIG T
SAT	.03399	3.9540E-03	.65560	8.595	.0000
(CONSTANT)	.23974	.31642		.758	.4505

```
------------ VARIABLES NOT IN THE EQUATION ------------
```

VARIABLE	BETA IN	PARTIAL	MIN TOLER	T	SIG T
EXTRA	.10679	.13313	.88622	1.323	.1890
SES	-.05341	-.06618	.87529	-.653	.5152
HSGPA	.33362	.41092	.86505	4.439	.0000

`* * * * * * * * * * * * * * * * * * * * * * * * *`

VARIABLE(S) ENTERED ON STEP NUMBER 2..   HSGPA   HIGH SCHOOL GRADE POINT AVERAGE

```
MULTIPLE R            .72532      ANALYSIS OF VARIANCE
R SQUARE              .52610                       DF    SUM OF SQUARES    MEAN SQUARE
ADJUSTED R SQUARE     .51632      REGRESSION        2       19.46028        9.73014
STANDARD ERROR        .42511      RESIDUAL         97       17.52972         .18072

                                  F =   53.84134      SIGNIF F =  .0000
```

------------ VARIABLES IN THE EQUATION ------------ | ------------ VARIABLES NOT IN THE EQUATION ------------

VARIABLE	B	SE B	BETA	T	SIG T		VARIABLE	BETA IN	PARTIAL	MIN TOLER	T	SIG T
SAT	.02763	3.8957E-03	.53305	7.093	.0000		EXTRA	.15787	.21361	.75053	2.142	.0347
HSGPA	.34232	.07711	.33362	4.439	.0000		SES	-.08086	-.10953	.75482	-1.080	.2830
(CONSTANT)	-.25281	.31046		-.814	.4175							

`* * * *  M U L T I P L E   R E G R E S S I O N  * * * *`

EQUATION NUMBER 1   DEPENDENT VARIABLE.. FGPA   FRESHMAN GRADE POINT AVERAGE

`* * * * * * * * * * * * * * * * * * * * * * * * * *`

VARIABLE(S) ENTERED ON STEP NUMBER 3..   EXTRA   EXTRACURRICULAR ACTIVITIES

```
MULTIPLE R            .74008      ANALYSIS OF VARIANCE
R SQUARE              .54772                       DF    SUM OF SQUARES    MEAN SQUARE
ADJUSTED R SQUARE     .53359      REGRESSION        3       20.26014        6.75338
STANDARD ERROR        .41746      RESIDUAL         96       16.72986         .17427

                                  F =   38.75255      SIGNIF F =  .0000
```

------------ VARIABLES IN THE EQUATION ------------ | ------------ VARIABLES NOT IN THE EQUATION ------------

VARIABLE	B	SE B	BETA	T	SIG T		VARIABLE	BETA IN	PARTIAL	MIN TOLER	T	SIG T
SAT	.02443	4.1071E-03	.47129	5.948	.0000		SES	-.03172	-.04145	.70682	-.404	.6868
HSGPA	.36608	.07653	.35677	4.783	.0000							
EXTRA	.05245	.02448	.15787	2.142	.0347							
(CONSTANT)	-.31918	.30644		-1.042	.3002							

FOR BLOCK NUMBER 1   PIN = 0.050 LIMITS REACHED.

Next, the regression coefficients or weights of the variable(s) in the model are given, both unstandardized (B) and standardized (BETA) weights, along with the standard error of estimate (SE B). These weights in the final model are used as multipliers of the values of the independent variables in the prediction equation. The significance level of each regression coefficient is given in the form of a *t*-test pitting the value obtained against a value of zero.

Finally, a table of the variables not yet in the equation (or having been removed from the equation) is given. A BETA weight is computed and given for each of these as if it were the next variable to be entered (BETA IN). The partial correlation coefficient (PARTIAL), the minimum tolerance level of the variable (if entered next), and the significance test value are also provided. The variable with the highest significant partial correlation coefficient will be entered on the next step.

Variables are entered (and removed) in a sequence of steps until all variables in the equation meet the criterion of statistical significance. Notice that the regression weights of the variables in the equation change as other variables are entered into the equation. The message "FOR BLOCK NUMBER 1 PIN=.050 LIMITS REACHED" notifies you that the final model has been constructed. With the present hypothetical data, the model would include as predictors (in order of importance): SAT, HSGPA, and EXTRA. The actual model, including the constant (intercept) value and the B weights, would be

FGPA = − .32 + .02 (SAT) + .37 (HSGPA) + .05 (EXTRA)

The three variables included in the model account for about 53 percent of the variance in FGPA as shown in the adjusted R^2 value.

EXAMPLE 2: PREDICTING FRESHMAN GRADE POINT AVERAGES—ADDITIONAL ANALYSES

To illustrate other aspects of the regression procedure, let us suppose that you wished to do the following:

1. Look at the analysis for a special subgroup—male subjects only
2. Use the method of mean substitution for missing data
3. Look at the best set of predictors for both FGPA and HSGPA.

Because your data have been saved in a system file called FGPA1, you may use the GET command to request the new analyses. For selecting a subgroup, REGRESSION has its own subcommand—SELECT. The possible relations are

EQ   Equal
NE   Not Equal
LT   Less than
GT   Greater than
LE   Less than or equal
GE   Greater than or equal

The command must appear prior to the VARIABLES= list to which it is to be applied. The SPSS^x file for these analyses is shown in Figure 12.6 and the output in Figure 12.7.

In Figure 12.7, you can see the means, standard deviations, and correlation matrix for the selected cases (SEX EQ 1 or male subjects). Note that no correlation can be computed for the variable SEX because it now has only one level. Step 1 of the regression analysis on FGPA shows SAT as the variable with the highest correlation with FGPA. Step 2 concludes the analysis for FGPA, producing as the final model:

FGPA = 1.42 + .03 (SAT) − .45 (HSTYPE)

A second dependent variable—HSGPA—was included in the RE-GRESSION command. Only one variable—HSTYPE—provided a significant level of prediction of HSGPA. FGPA was not tested as a predictor in that model according to the format of the DEPENDENT= subcommand. Thus the final model for HSGPA is

HSGPA = 3.23 − .36 (HSTYPE)

As noted on the printout, the mean substitution method for handling missing data was employed.

FIGURE 12.6 SPSS^x File for Additional Analyses on Freshman Grade Point Average Data

```
JOB. . .
EXEC SPSSX. . .              (JCL commands for your computer system)
TITLE  "SUBGROUP ANALYSIS ON FGPA DATA"
FILE HANDLE  FGPA1/local system specifications
GET  FILE=FGPA1
REGRESSION  SELECT SEX EQ 1/
            DESCRIPTIVES/
            MISSING=MEANSUBSTITUTION/
            VARIABLES=SEX TO FGPA/
            DEPENDENT=FGPA HSGPA/
            STEPWISE
FINISH
END OF JOB. . .             (JCL command for your computer system)
```

FIGURE 12.7 Output of Additional Analyses on Freshman Grade Point Average Data

SUBGROUP ANALYSIS ON FGPA DATA

**** M U L T I P L E   R E G R E S S I O N ****

VARIABLE LIST NUMBER 1   SUBSTITUTE MEAN FOR MISSING DATA

SELECTING ONLY CASES FOR WHICH SEX EQ 1

	MEAN	STD DEV	CASES	LABEL
SEX	1.000	.000	63	
HSTYPE	1.556	.501	63	HIGH SCHOOL TYPE
EXTRA	4.603	1.922	63	EXTRACURRICULAR ACTIVITIES
SES	4.365	1.726	63	SOCIOECONOMIC CLASS
SAT	75.651	12.364	63	SCHOLASTIC APTITUDE TEST PERFORMANCE
HSGPA	2.676	.540	63	HIGH SCHOOL GRADE POINT AVERAGE
FGPA	2.721	.604	63	FRESHMAN GRADE POINT AVERAGE

N OF CASES ENCOUNTERED = 63

MINIMUM (NON-ZERO) PAIRWISE N OF CASES = 63

CORRELATION:

'.' IS PRINTED IF A CORRELATION CANNOT BE COMPUTED.

	SEX	HSTYPE	EXTRA	SES	SAT	HSGPA	FGPA
SEX	1.000	.	.	.	.	.	.
HSTYPE	.	1.000	-.320	-.033	-.169	-.332	-.465
EXTRA	.	-.320	1.000	-.418	.244	-.113	.317
SES	.	-.033	-.418	1.000	-.247	.087	-.255
SAT	.	-.169	.244	-.247	1.000	.263	.604
HSGPA	.	-.332	-.113	.087	.263	1.000	.375
FGPA	.	-.465	.317	-.255	.604	.375	1.000

* * * * M U L T I P L E   R E G R E S S I O N * * * *

VARIABLE LIST NUMBER 1   SUBSTITUTE MEAN FOR MISSING DATA

SELECTING ONLY CASES FOR WHICH SEX EQ 1

EQUATION NUMBER 1   DEPENDENT VARIABLE..   FGPA   FRESHMAN GRADE POINT AVERAGE

DESCRIPTIVE STATISTICS ARE PRINTED ON PAGE   2

THE FOLLOWING 1 VARIABLES ARE CONSTANTS OR HAVE MISSING CORRELATIONS AND CAN NOT BE USED:
SEX

BEGINNING BLOCK NUMBER 1.   METHOD: STEPWISE

VARIABLE(S) ENTERED ON STEP NUMBER 1..   SAT   SCHOLASTIC APTITUDE TEST PERFORMANCE

MULTIPLE R	.60440	ANALYSIS OF VARIANCE		
R SQUARE	.36530		DF	SUM OF SQUARES	MEAN SQUARE
ADJUSTED R SQUARE	.35490	REGRESSION	1	8.25698	8.25698
STANDARD ERROR	.48496	RESIDUAL	61	14.34619	.23518

F =   35.10867   SIGNIF F = .0000

------------ VARIABLES IN THE EQUATION ------------

VARIABLE	B	SE B	BETA	T	SIG T
SAT	.02952	4.9812E-03	.60440	5.925	.0000
(CONSTANT)	.48779	.38176		1.278	.2062

----------- VARIABLES NOT IN THE EQUATION -----------

VARIABLE	BETA IN	PARTIAL	MIN TOLER	T	SIG T
HSTYPE	-.37383	-.46251	.97154	-4.041	.0002
EXTRA	.18044	.21965	.94055	1.744	.0863
SES	-.11252	-.13685	.93890	-1.070	.2889

* * * * M U L T I P L E   R E G R E S S I O N * * * *

EQUATION NUMBER 1   DEPENDENT VARIABLE..   FGPA   FRESHMAN GRADE POINT AVERAGE

VARIABLE(S) ENTERED ON STEP NUMBER 2..   HSTYPE   HIGH SCHOOL TYPE

MULTIPLE R	.70787	ANALYSIS OF VARIANCE		
R SQUARE	.50108		DF	SUM OF SQUARES	MEAN SQUARE
ADJUSTED R SQUARE	.48444	REGRESSION	2	11.32590	5.66295
STANDARD ERROR	.43354	RESIDUAL	60	11.27727	.18795

F =   30.12937   SIGNIF F = .0000

continued

FIGURE 12.7 (Continued)

```
-------------- VARIABLES IN THE EQUATION --------------        -------------- VARIABLES NOT IN THE EQUATION --------------

VARIABLE         B          SE B        BETA        T      SIG T     VARIABLE    BETA IN    PARTIAL    MIN TOLER       T     SIG T

SAT            .02644    4.5178E-03     .54134    5.851    .0000      EXTRA      -.07601    .09982     .86042        .771    .4440
HSTYPE        -.45063     .11152       -.37383   -4.041    .0002      SES        -.14321   -.19585     .90757      -1.534    .1304
(CONSTANT)    1.42175     .41218                   3.449    .0010
```

FOR BLOCK NUMBER   1   PIN = 0.050 LIMITS REACHED.

* * * *   M U L T I P L E   R E G R E S S I O N   * * * *

EQUATION NUMBER 2   DEPENDENT VARIABLE.. HSGPA   HIGH SCHOOL GRADE POINT AVERAGE

DESCRIPTIVE STATISTICS ARE PRINTED ON PAGE   2

THE FOLLOWING 1 VARIABLES ARE CONSTANTS OR HAVE MISSING CORRELATIONS AND CAN NOT BE USED:
     SEX

BEGINNING BLOCK NUMBER   1.   METHOD: STEPWISE

VARIABLE(S) ENTERED ON STEP NUMBER   1..   HSTYPE   HIGH SCHOOL TYPE

```
MULTIPLE R           .33217          ANALYSIS OF VARIANCE
R SQUARE             .11034                                DF      SUM OF SQUARES     MEAN SQUARE
ADJUSTED R SQUARE    .09575          REGRESSION             1          1.99207          1.99207
STANDARD ERROR       .51314          RESIDUAL              61         16.06221           .26331

                     F =   7.56536         SIGNIF F =   .0078
```

```
-------------- VARIABLES IN THE EQUATION --------------        -------------- VARIABLES NOT IN THE EQUATION --------------

VARIABLE         B          SE B        BETA        T      SIG T     VARIABLE    BETA IN    PARTIAL    MIN TOLER       T     SIG T

HSTYPE        -.35786     .13011       -.33217   -2.751    .0078      EXTRA      -.24488   -.24596     .89751      -1.966    .0540
(CONSTANT)    3.23286     .21246                  15.216    .0000      SES         .07650    .08106     .99890        .630    .5311
                                                                      SAT         .21298    .22256     .97154       1.768    .0821
```

FOR BLOCK NUMBER   1   PIN = 0.050 LIMITS REACHED.

OTHER ANALYSES AVAILABLE WITH REGRESSION

The REGRESSION procedure allows for several other choices related to the statistical analysis, the volume and contents of the output, and format of the output. For a complete description of all the variations available with the REGRESSION procedure, see the REGRESSION chapter in the *SPSS^x User's Guide*.

LIMITATIONS OF REGRESSION

If you exceed the workspace available on your computer system, either reduce the number of variables and/or analyses that you specify within a single REGRESSION command or consult your computer center staff.

13

Finding and Interpreting Errors

As you are learning how to use SPSS[x], you are likely to make a few mistakes. Instead of getting a completed analysis on your printout, you may receive some error messages that at times can be difficult to interpret if you are not familiar with the terminology. (Even experienced users get these messages from time to time.) The computer cannot always specify to you exactly what the problem is and often presents you with a rather cryptic message that is difficult to decipher.

It will be helpful if you keep in mind that the computer is trying to follow a set of instructions that you have outlined in your job control and SPSS[x] commands. An error occurs when it is unable to carry out your instructions. For example, if you use a variable name in your procedure command that is spelled differently from the one in your DATA LIST command, the computer will not "recognize" this variable and consequently cannot perform the analysis. The first step, then, in figuring out what error you have made is to examine the printout to determine the point at which the program ceased to operate.

Your printout will give a listing of the commands as it attempts to carry them out. The error message will generally follow the command in which there is a mistake. The computer will continue to check for and list other errors in the program but will not perform the analysis. Sometimes the later errors are simply a function of the earlier error, and one correc-

FIGURE 13.1   SPSS^x Printout Containing SPSS^x Error Messages

```
 1  0           TITLE    "MARKETING SURVEY OF JACK'S RESTAURANT"
 2  0           DATA LIST   /AGE 5-6 INCOME 8-12 PARTY 14-15 MEALR 17-18 MEALFF 20-21
 3  0                       MEALJ 23-24

THE ABOVE DATA LIST STATEMENT WILL READ   1 RECORDS FROM FILE INLINE

            VARIABLE   REC  START    END         FORMAT  WIDTH  DEC

            AGE          1     5       6          F        2     0
            INCOME       1     8      12          F        5     0
            PARTY        1    14      15          F        2     0
            MEALR        1    17      18          F        2     0
            MEALFF       1    20      21          F        2     0
            MEALJ        1    23      24          F        2     0

END OF DATALIST TABLE.

 4  0           VARIABLE LABELS   AGE "AGE OF RESPONDENTS"
 5  0                             INCOME "INCOME OF RESPONDENTS"
 6  0                             PARTI "NUMBER IN PARTY"
>WARNING  4461  LINE   6, COLUMN 19, TEXT: PARTI
>AN UNKNOWN VARIABLE NAME WAS SPECIFIED ON THE VAR LABELS COMMAND.   THE NAME
>AND THE LABEL WILL BE IGNORED.

 7  0                             MEALR "NUMBER MEALS AT A RESTAURANT"
 8  0                             MEALFF "NUMBER MEALS AT A FAST-FOOD RESTAURANT"
 9  0                             MEALJ "NUMBER OF MEALS AT JACK'S"
10  0           CONDESCRIPTIVE   AGES TO MEALJ


>ERROR     701  LINE  10, COLUMN 18, TEXT: AGES
>AN UNDEFINED VARIABLE NAME, OR A SCRATCH OR SYSTEM VARIABLE WAS SPECIFIED IN A
>VARIABLE LIST WHICH ACCEPTS ONLY STANDARD VARIABLES.   CHECK SPELLING, AND
>VERIFY THE EXISTENCE OF THIS VARIABLE.
>THIS COMMAND NOT EXECUTED.

11  0           STATISTICS   9 13
```

tion may be sufficient. Figure 13.1 is an illustration of a printout containing such errors. There are two errors in this program. The first error is the spelling of PARTI in the VARIABLE LABELS command instead of PAR-TY (as specified in the DATA LIST command). This error is actually a warning, and as such, it will not prevent execution of your program. It will, however, affect the labeling of variable PARTY on the printout. The second error, which will prevent the program from being executed, is the use of AGES in the CONDESCRIPTIVE statement instead of AGE (as specified in the DATA LIST command).

There are several general types of errors that are commonly made. We would like to discuss three of these briefly.

1. Errors related to your local computer system
2. Errors in your SPSS^x file that are detected by the SPSS^x program package
3. Errors in your SPSS^x file that are not detected by the SPSS^x program package

ERRORS RELATED TO YOUR LOCAL COMPUTER SYSTEM

One problem that may arise concerns the storage capacity of your local computer. Sometimes this capacity is smaller than that specified in the limitations of SPSS^x (i.e., in the number of variables and computations allowed). In that case, you will receive a message from your local system to the effect that you have requested too many variables or exceeded the space limitations of the system. As we have noted in the individual procedure chapters, you will need to find a reasonable way to reduce your request (e.g., by cutting down on the number of variables or computations you have specified).

Other problems may occur with regard to your use of the job control language. If you have made mistakes in your JCL commands (e.g., misspelled your account name or left out an important parameter), your SPSS^x program will not run. Similarly, you may make mistakes using the procedures for creating, editing, storing, and accessing files in your local computer system. Here we can only recommend that you consult persons knowledgeable about your specific computer system and its operation because systems vary from one installation to another. It is important, though, for you to recognize whether your error is a local system error or an SPSS^x error.

ERRORS DETECTED BY SPSS^x

If any of your SPSS^x commands deviate from the required format, you will receive an error message and usually will not be able to run your program to its conclusion. This includes errors of spelling (e.g., DATA LEST instead of DATA LIST), errors of spacing or location (e.g., DATALIST instead of DATA LIST), and errors of punctuation (e.g., using periods instead of commas or spaces in a list of variables). Failure to include all of the required elements of a command (e.g., parentheses, slashes) will similarly result in error messages. (There is some latitude in the required format of certain SPSS^x commands, but while learning SPSS^x, you are better off following the exact format given.)

SPSS^x will also detect errors of program logic or inconsistencies within the commands you have entered. Some fairly frequent errors include

1. *Noncorrespondence of variable names in different parts of the program.* If you use a variable name anywhere in the program (e.g., in VARIABLE LABELS or VALUE LABELS commands or in procedure statements), it must be spelled exactly as it appears in the DATA LIST command. Furthermore, *all* variables used in the program must be contained in the DATA LIST command unless they result from transformation commands such as COMPUTE. If not, the program is searching for something that does not exist, and it cannot proceed any further.
2. *Inappropriate characters in the data lines.* If you have indicated that variables are coded numerically, any deviation from that will be detected as an error. The most frequent such error that we encounter is the typing in of the alphabetic character *O* instead of the numeric character *0*. In addition, remember that SPSS^x reads blank fields as missing values and not as zeros.
3. *Failure to precede the data lines with a BEGIN DATA statement and follow the data*

lines with an END DATA statement. When the Within-File Method of data entry is used, these two statements must be included in your SPSSˣ file. If you forget to include the BEGIN DATA statement, the computer will try to read your data lines as SPSSˣ commands, and it will not be able to interpret or recognize them. Similarly, if you fail to include an END DATA statement, the computer will try to read the SPSSˣ commands following the data lines as data lines. In either case, you will get an SPSSˣ error message.

4. *Exceeding SPSSˣ limitations.* Each procedure has its own limits in terms of numbers of variables and computations that can be requested. For example, a maximum of five dependent variables can be specified in a single ANOVA command. In this case, your error message will inform you that some limits of storage have been exceeded by your requests. As we have said before, reduce the size of your requests by using alternative formats. The limitations section at the end of each chapter should be helpful here.

ERRORS THAT SPSSˣ CANNOT DETECT

SPSSˣ cannot detect many of the errors that you may make in typing your data lines. For example, if you type in the wrong number, it will obviously not be detected by the computer (unless you had specified an alphabetic character and you typed a number or vice versa). Thus, you need to proofread your data for accuracy.

Another error that is generally not detected by SPSSˣ is the placement of data in the wrong columns (as compared with the locations specified in the DATA LIST command). For example, if you have specified that VARA is in columns 3 and 4 and then you type it inadvertently in columns 4 and 5, the computer will read what is in columns 3 and 4 and perform the analyses on these values—incorrectly.

One way to detect this type of error is to use the LIST procedure, which is described in Chapter 3. This procedure will create a printout of your data, according to the format specified on your DATA LIST command. This listing is useful for checking whether your data have been read according to the specifications on your DATA LIST command. Another way to detect such errors is to check the descriptive statistics on the printout (e.g., the means) and see if they make sense. If possible, calculate the means by hand and compare them with those on your printout. If that is impractical because of large data sets, at least make sure that the number of cases is reported accurately and/or that descriptive statistics are reasonable with regard to the scales, scores, or categories being used.

ONE FINAL WARNING

Knowing SPSSˣ is no substitute for knowing statistics. Eliminating all the previously mentioned errors from your SPSSˣ program does not guarantee that you have used SPSSˣ *appropriately.* Rather, some background in statistics is a prerequisite for appropriate and effective use of SPSS^x. An understanding of experimental and statistical methods will enable you to select the correct statistical procedures for your data, determine whether your data satisfy the assumptions of your statistical tests, and interpret the results of your statistical procedures.

14

Additional Capabilities of SPSS^x

In this book we have intentionally covered commonly used and relatively straightforward procedures. The SPSS^x program package, however, has extensive and varied capabilities. As you become a proficient user of SPSS^x, you will probably want to examine these other capabilities. In this chapter we will outline other procedures and capacities that are available with SPSS^x. We encourage you to explore these options in further detail as you need them. (The specifics for these other commands are available in the latest release of the *SPSS^x User's Guide*.)

First we would like to present the INFO command, because it will enable you to obtain information about recent changes and new additions to the SPSS^x system and also information about specific command formats for your particular computer system. Second, we present brief descriptions of some of the statistical procedures available with SPSS^x that are not covered in this book. Finally, we will point out a few additional capabilities of the SPSS^x program package.

THE INFO COMMAND

The INFO command can be used to

1. Obtain specific information for running SPSS^x on your local computer system. Occasionally, we have not been able to give information about a particu-

lar command because of variation from one computer system to another. This is true of the FILE HANDLE command, for example, in which local system specifications are usually required. To find out how to construct these local system specifications for your particular computer, you can ask people who are familiar with using SPSS^x on your computer or you can request additional information with the INFO command.

2. Obtain updated information on SPSS^x. From time to time, SPSS^x commands and procedures are modified or new ones are added. The INFO command will enable you to find out about these changes. Although this manual describes the most recent version of SPSS^x (Release 2.1), there will undoubtedly be new releases, and you can keep abreast of these changes with the INFO command.

Keywords are used along with the INFO command to request certain types of documentation. These keywords and their functions are shown in Figure 14.1. To access information, type the word INFO and then type the keyword(s) that represents the documentation that you want. The INFO command and all keywords included on it must be separated by at least one space. For example

```
INFO  LOCAL
INFO  CONDESCRIPTIVE
INFO  OVERVIEW LOCAL PROCEDURES
INFO  ALL
```

FIGURE 14.1 Subcommands Available with the INFO Command

KEYWORD	DESCRIPTION
OVERVIEW	This keyword provides you with an overview or "table of contents" of the information available to you with the INFO command.
LOCAL	This keyword requests information that is pertinent to using SPSS^x on your computer system. Among other things, it provides you with information about the JCL (*job control language*) commands and local system specifications for the FILE HANDLE command.
FACILITIES	This keyword requests updated information about the most recent version of SPSS^x. When sufficient modifications and additions to the SPSS^x program package are warranted, new versions or releases of SPSS^x are created and installed in computer systems. The FACILITIES keyword will describe the changes that have been made (for all commands except the procedure commands) in the most recent release.
PROCEDURES	This keyword will provide you with modifications to *all* procedures in the most recent release of SPSS^x.
CONDESCRIPTIVE PEARSON CORR, and so on	If you wish to know about changes in specific procedures (rather than all of the procedures), then you can request these procedures by name. A slash must follow the name of each procedure when more than one is listed.
ALL	Using the keyword ALL is a short cut for requesting OVERVIEW, LOCAL, FACILITIES, and PROCEDURES. You should be somewhat cautious in your use of this keyword because it may result in a large amount of output.

FIGURE 14.2   Example of SPSS^x File Using the INFO Command

```
JOB. . .
EXEC SPSSX. . .            (JCL commands for your computer system)
INFO  LOCAL T-TEST/CONDESCRIPTIVE
FINISH
END OF JOB. . .           (JCL command for your computer system)
```

In addition, the names of specific *procedures* must be separated by a slash (/). For example

```
INFO  OVERVIEW LOCAL CONDESCRIPTIVE/T-TEST
INFO  CONDESCRIPTIVE/T-TEST/PEARSON CORR/ANOVA
```

The INFO command can be typed within any SPSS^x file as long as it occurs after the initial JCL commands, before the FINISH command, and not between the BEGIN DATA and END DATA commands (when used).

You may initially want to write an SPSS^x file for the sole purpose of getting information about SPSS^x on your local computer system. As shown in Figure 14.2, no procedure command is needed in this file.

OTHER STATISTICAL PROCEDURES AVAILABLE WITH SPSS^x

In this section, you will find brief descriptions of some additional SPSS^x procedures. Generally, this will not be enough information for you to run the procedure, but it will allow you to determine whether the procedure would be useful to you. If you wish to find out more about a particular procedure, look under the appropriate command name in the index of the most recent *SPSS^x User's Guide* or request information with the INFO command.

AGGREGATE Procedure

The AGGREGATE command and related subcommands represent the SPSS^x procedure for clustering cases into specified groups for further analysis on the groups (aggregates). For example, if you had obtained demographic data on a large number of registered voters in a particular city, you might wish to look at the data by precinct groupings, obtaining averages for each variable to be compared among the precincts. That is, instead of a single voter being a case, a new file is constructed using the precinct (aggregate grouping) as a case. Summary values (e.g., means, sums) are used to represent the variables being compared across the aggregate groups. Thus you might compare such factors as average income, average family size, and average length of residence among precinct groupings. Several functions are available for comparing aggregate data in addition to means and sums.

MULT RESPONSE Procedure

This procedure is used to represent data when individual variables may have more than one value. For example, questionnaires often contain items that allow the respondent to "check all that apply." You might ask a person to view a list and to check all symptoms experienced in the last 24 hours. The person might check several symptoms and leave others blank. Similarly, respondents may be asked to rank order the possible responses to a particular question—for example, magazines preferred for leisure reading. Such variables cannot be appropriately analyzed with the CROSSTABS or FREQUENCIES procedures, but with MULT RESPONSE, crosstabulation and frequency tables can be obtained and displayed.

BREAKDOWN Procedure

The BREAKDOWN procedure is used when one wishes to obtain means and variances for dependent variables according to the levels or values of the independent variables. That is, one may request lists or tables of means and variances for each level of each independent variable or combinations of the independent variables. The procedure also allows you to obtain a one-way analysis of variance for a given independent variable. For example, if you measured typing speed (dependent variable) under two conditions of noise (low versus high) and three conditions of lighting (low, moderate, high), you could get a listing or table of the means and variances for typing speed for each of the six groups in the 2 by 3 design. You could, additionally, request a one-way analysis of variance on either of the two independent variables.

Although the same effects could be generated with a series of SELECT IF and CONDESCRIPTIVE commands, the BREAKDOWN procedure is the most efficient method for obtaining this information.

MANOVA Procedure

The MANOVA procedure enables you to perform univariate and multivariate analyses of variance and covariance. It is an extensive and flexible program useful for a variety of experimental designs (e.g., nested designs, randomized block designs, split-plot designs, Latin squares designs). It is also appropriate for within-subjects (i.e., repeated measures) and mixed designs involving one or more independent variables. Numerous statistical tests are available with this procedure, including those typically associated with general linear models (e.g., multivariate regressions, discriminant function coefficients, and canonical correlations). Output may be obtained in both tabular and graphic format.

LOGLINEAR Procedure

This procedure is employed with nominal data, that is, variables whose values are categories rather than ordinal ranks or scales. The defining characteristic of nominal data is that the categories differ in quality and not quantity. For example, if one variable was voting choice (Candidate A, B, or C) and one variable was voter's region of the country (North, South, East, or West), you would be dealing with nominal data. The purpose of the LOGLINEAR procedure is to enable model fitting and hypothesis testing when nominal data are involved in the model. Continuous variables may be incorporated in the models as covariates. Several model-testing procedures are available with LOGLINEAR. Further, the results of your analysis may be displayed in both tabular and graphic format.

PARTIAL CORR Procedure

The PARTIAL CORR procedure allows you to examine correlations among certain variables while controlling for the effects of other variables. That is, you could look at the residual correlation of blood pressure with age after the variance contributed by weight has been accounted for. For the set of variables involved, you obtain both a Pearson product-moment correlation matrix and the designated partial correlation coefficients with significance levels.

DISCRIMINANT Procedure

The DISCRIMINANT procedure deals with linear combinations of variables and tests the ability of certain combinations of variables to distinguish subgroups of cases. That is, the program would identify the best linear combination of variables to separate cases into specified subgroups (e.g., males and females). Either you may choose the direct-entry method of variable inclusion in the analysis or you may use one of five stepwise entry methods. Discriminant function coefficients are calculated for prediction of group membership.

FACTOR Procedure

The FACTOR procedure is used for principal component analysis and factor analysis of data. Because these types of statistical analysis are complicated, the FACTOR procedure should not be employed without a reasonable understanding of the assumptions underlying the choices involved (e.g., regarding factor extraction techniques and factor rotation). Numerous subcommands provide a variety of options for carrying out the statistical techniques as well as for formatting and displaying the results.

NONPAR CORR Procedure

This procedure is used to perform correlational tests on ordinal scale (i.e., rank order) data. When your data are in the form of ordinal measures, the traditional Pearson product-moment correlation test (computed with the PEARSON CORR procedure) is inappropriate. Instead, you should use either or both of the following tests, and these are requested with the NONPAR CORR procedure: Spearman's rho and Kendall's tau *b*. A correlation matrix is produced containing the requested type of correlation coefficients along with significance levels.

NPAR TESTS Procedure

By using this procedure, you can access a variety of nonparametric tests. Nonparametric tests require fewer assumptions about the distribution of your scores and can be used with nominal (categorical) or ordinal (rank) data. Tests available with this procedure are chi-square, runs, binomial, McNemar, Cochran Q, Kolmogorov-Smirnov, sign, Wilcoxin, Kendall coefficient of concordance, Freidman two-way Anova, median, Mann-Whitney, Wold-Wolfowitz, Moses, and Kruskall-Wallis. With each test, appropriate additional parameters and options are designated by the user.

BOX-JENKINS Procedure

This statistical procedure is used to compare time series data with a set of statistical models to test for goodness of fit and to obtain projections or forecasts. The results may be printed or plotted in a variety of ways.

RELIABILITY Procedure

The RELIABILITY procedure allows you to do two kinds of analysis: (1) item analysis on data from multi-item additive scales (e.g., attitude scales) and (2) analysis of variance for several kinds of repeated measures designs (including appropriate statistical tests such as Tukey's test for additivity and Hotelling's T). For item analysis, the RELIABILITY procedure provides options for five basic models and a variety of related coefficients of reliability. In addition, summary statistics for variables and scales may be obtained as well as inter-item correlations. A special feature among the analysis of variance capacities of this procedure is analysis of variance for dichotomous data (variables having only two values) using Cochran's Q test.

SURVIVAL Procedure

This is a fairly specialized procedure. It is used predominantly in medical research, with dependent variables representing the time from some initial point of origin (e.g., onset of illness) to some terminal point (e.g., death). The program output consists of life tables, along with survival functions, plots of survival functions, and comparisons among subgroups.

OTHER CAPABILITIES OF THE SPSSˣ PROGRAM PACKAGE

SPSSˣ is rapidly adding new features to its already extensive set of capabilities. You will be able to keep up with these features by following updated releases of the *SPSSˣ User's Guide* and by using the INFO command. Here we would like to point out two programs that you will find quite helpful for preparing research reports and presentation materials. These are the REPORT procedure and SPSS Graphics.

REPORT Procedure

The REPORT procedure enables you to format the presentation of data and statistics in tabular form, controlling such things as page length, margins, vertical spacing, page titles and footnotes, and labels for variables and statistics. The procedure also allows you to obtain some of the same descriptive statistics and summary tables found in CONDESCRIPTIVE, FREQUENCIES, and BREAKDOWN as well as some additional statistics. Its basic purpose is to allow the user to control the arrangement of descriptive output to correspond to a formal report style.

SPSS Graphics

With the SPSS Graphics program, you can obtain piecharts, barcharts, and/or line graphs with full labels and comments. Your computer facility must have the appropriate graphics printing equipment in order for you to use this attractive form of output. With the proper equipment, you are offered a variety of color and format options for the plotting of your data.

It is possible that your computer system cannot or does not accommodate all of the procedures we have mentioned in this chapter. Some of them require extensive storage capabilities or special equipment. Most of the procedures, however, are likely to be available to you. Now that you have learned the basic logic of accessing and using SPSSˣ, you should have little difficulty advancing to the *SPSSˣ User's Guide*. We encourage you to experiment with the range of possibilities that SPSSˣ has to offer for data analysis and presentation.

Index

Commands in an SPSS^x File

NAME OF COMMAND	FUNCTION
TITLE	Provides a title for your printout.
DATA LIST	Tells the computer the names of your variables and the column locations for each variable. This command is required unless you are accessing an SPSS^x system file.
MISSING VALUES	Allows you to designate a code for missing data.
SET	Allows you to assign values to blank fields in your data set.
VARIABLE LABELS	Allows you to give more descriptive names to your variables. These will appear on the printout in addition to the abbreviated versions of the variable names in the DATA LIST command.
VALUE LABELS	Allows you to give descriptive labels to the different values or levels of your variables.
COMMENT	Enables you to place reminders and descriptions within your SPSS^x file.
RECODE	Allows you to change the codes or values of your variables.
COMPUTE	Allows you to perform computations on your data to create new variables.
IF	Specifies logical contingencies (e.g., greater than, equal to, less than) for creating new variables.
SELECT IF	Allows you to select certain cases or subjects for analysis and to eliminate others.
TEMPORARY	Specifies that data transformations (made with the RECODE, COMPUTE, IF, and SELECT IF commands) are temporary and apply only to the procedure that immediately follows the transformations.
LIST procedure	Causes a listing of your data to be printed.
Procedure command (e.g., ANOVA or PEARSON CORR)	Defines the particular statistical analysis to be performed.
OPTIONS	Specifies which, if any, of several choices are to be applied to the selected procedure. The available options are listed with the descriptions of the procedures.
STATISTICS	Specifies additional statistics to be performed along with the basic procedure. These choices are listed with the descriptions of the procedures.
BEGIN DATA	Tells the computer that the next line it reads is the first data line. This command must be used with the Within-File Method of reading data.
Data lines	Used in the Within-File Method of reading data. At least one line for each subject or case is presented here for the computer to read.
END DATA	Tells the computer that the last data line has been read. This command is required when using the Within-File Method of reading data.
FINISH	This is the last of the SPSS^x commands, and it indicates to the computer that the SPSS^x file is complete. This command is optional, but we suggest that you use it.

File Communication Commands

FILE HANDLE	Provides a brief name for files that are to be stored or accessed. This command is required whenever you want to read information from and/or create other files.
SAVE	Tells the computer to store the data in an SPSS^x system file for future use. This file can later be retrieved with the GET command.
GET	Tells the computer to access an SPSS^x system file. Once the file is accessed, you can request statistical analyses without retyping the data lines and control commands.